101
PITCHING
DRILLS

BOB BENNETT

ISBN: 1-58518-224-9
Library of Congress Catalog Card Number: 99-60465
Cover design and book layout: Paul Lewis
Cover Photos: Denis McElroy

Coaches Choice
P.O. Box 1828
Monterey, CA 93940
www.coacheschoice.com

This book is dedicated to Oliver Bidwell, who was one of the most successful high school coaches in the country, and to Pete Beiden, who was one of the most successful college coaches in the country. Both men were highly skilled students of the game and masters of the fundamentals of the game. I was fortunate to have played for both coaches.

Oliver Bidwell was my high school coach. Pete Beiden was my college coach. Their passion for the game ignited a fire in each of their players. Their knowledge and keen interest in the fundamentals of the game were passed on others. I and so many players were blessed to have played for these two dedicated coaches.

ACKNOWLEDGMENTS

The many pitchers I have coached made this book possible. Their dedication to learning and their willingness to explore new ideas helped to develop many of these drills. Each pitcher is unique. Although some have similar styles, use similar grips and have similar arm slots, no two are alike. Therefore the need to use a variety of drills is important. Often a particular drill dramatically helps one pitcher but does not affect another. This makes cooperation between the pitcher and the coach an absolute necessity if true teaching is to take place. So, I acknowledge and thank every pitcher who has allowed me to experiment, examine and adjust his pitching deliveries.

Teaching is a challenging adventure. Learning is similar. To do either, the mind must be free to explore and be willing to meet the challenges and gain from the adventure. Each pitcher offers a pitching coach opportunity to create a better road to communicating. Those pitchers who had difficulty understanding the mechanics of pitching were catalysts for innovation in drills. The highly skilled pitchers set examples and encouraged the use of the drills.

I owe a great debt of gratitude to the many coaches who passed on their knowledge of pitching to me. Many coaches filled this bill. Ollie Bidwell and Pete Beiden are at the head of the list. Though they did not write a word in this book, they are largely responsible for the information in it. To all those coaches whom I heard speak at clinics or who took time to discuss pitching with me, I salute. These coaches were the genesis of many of these drills.

CONTENTS

CHAPTER	DRILL #	PAGE #
1 Lower Body Mechanics	1-18	13
2 Middle Body Mechanics	19-25	35
3 Upper Body Mechanics	26-37	45
4 Improving Velocity	38-40	63
5 Improving Control	41-49	69
6 Fielding Skills	50-62	79
7 Pickoff Moves	63-68	93
8 Warming Up and Conditioning	69-86	101
9 Correcting Flaws	87-96	117
10 Stuff	97-101	133

The purpose of any baseball drill should be to improve either a given skill or the general skill level of the ball player who is performing the drill. A good drill should relate closely to the actual skill that will be used in live game action. No drill should be used simply to keep the player busy, and no drill should be used that does not relate to the game of baseball. A pitcher who understands the purpose of the drill he is about to perform, as well as the drill's carryover to live action, will be more apt to perform it successfully.

A successful drill should focus on improving one or more skills. The results of the drill should be evident in game situations. Since each drill should be designed to help the pitcher maximize his efficiency, each drill should be operated with attention to details.

Many baseball drills have been around for a long time. Most have been passed down from generation to generation. These so-called "standard drills" have been tested and have stood the test of time. Although they should be used generously, these "standard" drills—like any other drills—should be used only to service specific needs.

The most productive way to help the pitcher reach a well-conditioned state is through baseball-related running drills. These drills not only provide an excellent source of physical conditioning, but they also add to the general skill level of the pitcher. A drill that calls for the pitcher to cover first base, for example, requires running ability, an understanding of the necessary technique involved, and the proper timing. This sort of running is game related. Drills of this nature help to improve the fundamentals of base running and the fielding of bunts, ground balls, and fly balls. They are the best types of drills because they help the pitcher to develop his baseball skills and, in the process, help him to become well conditioned.

Coaches should keep in mind that any drill is only as good as the player and the coach make it. Drills are simply made up from parts of the game. It is the repetition of these drills, along with the pitcher's commitment to improve his skills, that make a drill successful. Any drill performed half-heartedly or casually will normally get poor results. On the other hand, almost any drill that is done with enthusiasm and commitment should deliver some pluses. Therefore, coaches should make sure that each drill has both a specific purpose and a specific desired outcome. Practice does not make perfect; rather, practice makes permanent.

Some drills require certain types of expensive equipment. If such equipment is available and the drills are effective with the equipment, then, by all means, coaches should use this equipment to their advantage. The mind, however, is probably the best source for inventing new drills. A drill will often require no equipment, or perhaps such simple equipment as a shoestring or a paper cup. In the end, it is people who make the drill effective, for even the best equipment will not enhance a pitcher's skill level if he is not committed to improving himself or if he fails to understand the drill's purpose.

Some of the best drills are designed out of necessity. Regardless of where these drills come from, it is important to design each drill so that it fits a particular need or occasion. As the season unfolds, the need for specific drills to fill specific needs will naturally arise.

All the drills in this book are practical. They can be used with pitchers of all age groups. Many of the drills do not require unusual or expensive equipment.

At times, a coach will face teaching dilemmas. In some instances, he will deliver his message, only to discover that his message has not been received. Other times, he will present the same message in a number of different ways, but to no avail—the player still doesn't quite grasp the importance of the coach's pointers. At times like these, when the coach sees that he is not getting through to the pitcher, he is left with two options: either give up on the player or persist in getting the player to understand and cooperate.

At a crossroads, the coach may find that he needs to improvise, to take a different course of action. He may, for example, decide to develop a lesson plan that deals only with a particular player. To be sure, a drill that fits that player's unique learning problems may be the answer to the player's problem. Regardless, the coach should be creative. By branching out and trying different methods, he will eventually develop some really good drills.

Many of the drills in this book were created on the spot. A good example is Drill #35 (Mat to Help Arm Angle), which was devised after one of my pitchers could not get his arm up into the proper throwing position. After I had used every known drill and given every explanation available, the pitcher still had the same problem. A simple on-the-spot drill solved this pitcher's problem. A conveyor belt mat was placed about 30 feet from the pitching rubber, toward home plate. The pitcher was told to bounce the ball on the hop to the catcher. To accomplish this task, he had to get his arm in the proper position. This simple drill did more than all the explanations and other drills combined.

In summation, if the drills presented in this book enhance the ability of young men to take better advantage of their natural abilities and talent, then the time and energy required to write this book will have been well worth the effort.

DEVELOPING A PITCHING LANGUAGE

Developing a pitching language is extremely important to the learning process. The use of words will have little or no meaning to the pitcher if the words are not understood clearly—like speaking Chinese to an Egyptian. Therefore, coaches should develop a language filled with pitching words. These words should be strong in enhancement recall. Strong words or terms may bring back memories or help the pitcher flash to a specific scene or serve as a reminder to him to review important lessons of the past.

Words or phrases that emphasize discipline should help the pitcher get right to the point. These words may describe vividly the fundamental that the pitcher needs to stress. They may add clarity and simplification to the task at hand. They may cause the pitcher to see clearly, to understand exactly, and to discard distractions that are impeding his learning. Words and phrases that suggest and imply positive actions are also important, because they flash to the pitcher's mind a picture of possibilities and probabilities. In turn, they help to create improvement and commitment in the pitcher.

Before he studies the pitching system his coach is employing, the pitcher should understand the language that will be used. This language will be his vehicle for knowledge. Short statements or words that are clearly understood serve to get the message across to him quickly. Many times, a good explanation is one that is short and to the point.

If the pitcher is only slightly off course, he may require only a phrase or a word to right him. If the word or phrase is strong, understandable, creates a clear picture, and points to the problem at hand, the easier it should be for the pitcher to correct his flaws. The time spent by the coach both in the demonstration and the definition of the pitching language will pay dividends for the pitcher.

DEFINITION OF TERMS

The following words and phrases make up the pitching language. We have developed this language in the course of several years. Since learning is a perpetual process, changes and new descriptions are added each year to the pitching vocabulary. The language, however, still remains relatively constant and should withstand the test of time.

→ *Back knee down.* This term refers to the pitcher's push-off knee driving toward the ground as his push-off foot drives from the pitching rubber.

→ *Balance drills.* This term describes a series of movements designed to help the pitcher develop the proper balance. The drills include work with both the pitcher's stride foot and his push-off foot and can be done with or without his throwing the baseball.

→ *Belly button to target.* At the beginning stages of the pitcher's windup, and as his push-off foot is placed on the rubber, his belly button should face the target. As his chest and head reach out to throw, his belly button should also face the target. If the pitcher's belly button is not in this position during these two phases, he will have to make extra movements and undue adjustments in order to correct the position of his body.

→ *Bent front leg.* The pitcher's stride leg should be bent during his leg lift and remain bent through both his push-off and his stride. As his throwing arm finishes the last phases of his throwing motion, his front leg should be bent, with the knee of that leg pointed inward.

→ *Bouncing hands.* This term refers to the action prior to the pitcher's hand separation. A slight lift of his hands shortly before his hands separate should create an opportunity to develop the proper rhythm as his hands prepare for the throw. The bouncing action should not cover more than a few inches. This movement should help his pitching arm drop, reach back, pick up, and get to the top of the throwing arc with freedom and quickness.

→ *Break the hands softly.* This term is another way of describing the pitcher's hand separation. His hands should be soft and relaxed as they separate. Relaxation and softness at this point should help the pitcher to better control both of his arms as they prepare for the throw.

→ *Chest out.* This term describes the chest as it extends toward the target during the pitcher's throwing motion. The pitcher should assume a barrel chest and arched-back position as he reaches to throw. Instructing the pitcher to "stick your chest out" or "throw your breasts at the target" are also effective ways of illustrating the proper method for this maneuver. The pitcher's breasts should also be level as they are thrown toward his target.

→ *Concave chest.* This is a negative term. It indicates that both the pitcher's throwing-arm shoulder and his front shoulder are squeezing toward each other. This action is inclined to shorten the pitcher's throwing arm and cause his arm to suddenly stop. The concave-chest action is one of the major reasons for recoiling. This action is restrictive and may result in severe injury to the pitcher's shoulder, his elbow, and his back.

→ *Deactivate bottom of stride leg.* This term describes the first part of the pitcher's stride. The pitcher should hold his lift leg up and avoid thrusting with the bottom half of that leg. He should try to get the feel of not using the bottom of his stride leg until just a few inches prior to the landing of his stride foot. Overuse of the stride leg can cause the pitcher a multitude of problems, including overstriding, opening too soon, recoiling, breaking his rhythm, and prematurely expending his power.

→ *Downward angle.* This term describes the direction that the pitcher's throwing arm should travel after it assumes its maximum height. It also describes the direction the ball should travel as it leaves the pitcher's hand. The pitcher should feel as though he is throwing downhill. This term also reminds the pitcher to get on top of the ball.

→ *Elevate the front hip.* At the top of the pitcher's leg lift, his front hip should be higher than his back hip. From a side view, the pitcher's belt line should be higher on his glove-hand side than on his throwing-arm side. This action should improve the pitcher's pivot and coiling position and enhance his stride. It should not cause the back shoulder to drop. The shoulders should remain relatively level.

→ *Eyes to target.* This term is used to remind the pitcher to reach toward the target with his head. This action should help him to keep his head aligned with his target. If both of his eyes are focused directly on his target, the rest of his body should follow. This motion will also create better extension with the pitcher's throwing arm.

→ *Fingers down.* This term refers to the position of the pitcher's fingers as his pitching hand separates from his glove, as well as the position of his fingers as his pitching arm is lifted in preparation for his throw. The pitcher's fingertips should be pointed toward the ground during this movement. This action should help him get his arm up to the top of the arc without undue strain and also properly prepare his wrist for its duties.

→ *Forward wrist.* This term refers to the position of the pitcher's wrist at the top of his throwing motion. His wrist at this point in his delivery should be in a cocked or ready position, which should allow for the full snap of his wrist as his arm is brought forward to release the ball. This action should prevent the pitcher from slinging, or pushing, the ball. His forward wrist should be in a relaxed position, ready to move backward quickly, and then snap forward to complete a full wrist snap at the end of his release point.

→ *Front arm (take out and bring in).* This term describes the method in which the pitcher's front arm is used as his throwing motion is executed. "Taking it out" implies a controlled movement, which is precisely the proper movement. "Bringing it in" should paint a picture of the arm as guided, or drawn back in, rather than jerked back. These actions create rhythmical movements and eliminate uncontrolled activities.

→ *Inside to inside.* This term is used to illustrate a properly balanced position. While in his stretch-position stance, the pitcher should keep his weight balanced between the inside of his back foot and the inside of his stride foot. His push-off should be executed from the inside of his push-off foot, and his stride should be made with his weight transferring to the inside of his front foot. This term is also used when the pitcher is in his stationary stride position. In that case, the pitcher should transfer his weight from the inside of one foot to the inside of the other.

→ *Inward knee.* This term refers to the back knee of the pitcher during his push-off placement on the pitching rubber and also during the beginning of his driving action for his push-off. It also refers to the position of the pitcher's knee as his stride foot lands and as his weight is placed on his foot to complete his throw. An inward knee at each of these points should encourage both a more forceful push-off and a proper balance with his stride and follow-through.

→ *Lead with the hip.* This term describes the beginning of the pitcher's stride. His front hip should move first and drive toward his stride spot, as well as toward his target. This movement should create a greater thrust and propel his body in the direction of the target. The pitcher should get the feel of striding with his hip.

→ *Leg lift.* This term refers to the movement of the pitcher's front leg in aiding his coiling action and preparing for his stride. The leg lift should be controlled. It should not be a swinging or slinging action.

→ *Level eyes.* This term describes the proper position of the pitcher's eyes at the beginning of, during, and at the end of his throwing motion. Keeping his eyes level with his target ensures a proper angle and improves the direction of his body parts toward the target as well. Level eyes should prevent the pitcher's head from tilting.

→ *Locked knees.* The pitcher's legs are straight, with no bending at his knees.

→ *On top of the ball.* This term refers to the position of the pitcher's fingers as they grip the ball. This position encourages a proper angle at the top of his throw, and his fingers should be on top of the ball at this point. This term can also describe the correct position of the pitcher as he lifts the ball up into the proper throwing position. It is also used to describe the proper position of the pitcher's fingers when he throws a curveball and the position of his fingers as they aid in a better release of a particular pitch.

→ *Push-off.* The push-off is the activity of driving off the rubber. The total act includes the pushing action of the pitcher's push-off foot and the lead action with his front hip. It also includes keeping his lift leg up as long as possible.

→ *Release point below the bill of the cap.* The proper feel for the release of the ball should be below the bill of the pitcher's cap and well out and directly in front of his eyes. The ball should not actually be released from that point, however. The actual release should be much sooner. The benefit of this feel is that the pitcher should be able to stay on top of the ball, get the maximum use of his fingers, and develop a sense of feel for the direction of his throw.

→ *Right to left (RHP).* This term describes the route of the pitcher's arm as it proceeds through his throwing motion. His arm should properly extend toward his target and travel in a right-to-left action in front of his body. This motion should allow the pitcher's throwing arm to continue through the arc with freedom and also permit a full follow-through, with the elbow of his throwing arm touching against the outside of his stride-leg thigh.

→ *Separation of hands.* This term deals with the separation of the pitcher's hands in both the stretch and the windup positions. The separation is also referred to as the breaking of the hands. The pitcher should develop a consistent point for his separation. This point should be the same from both the windup and the stretch. This consistency is important to his throw, because it really marks the beginning of his throwing motion.

→ *Soft out of the glove.* This term describes how the pitcher's hands should properly separate. As his pitching hand leaves his glove, it should be soft and relaxed. A soft and relaxed separation creates a faster arm movement. This action should help his pitching arm get up into the proper throwing position with speed and ease. This action should also improve the movement of both the pitcher's glove hand and his arm.

→ *Toe ahead of heel.* This term refers to the correct position of the pitcher's push-off foot when he places it on or in front of the pitching rubber to begin his throwing motion. It also refers to his stride foot as it is planted, as well as the finish of his follow-through. The toe ahead of the heel enhances the pitcher's thrust and helps him maintain proper balance.

→ *Unlocked knees.* This term indicates a slight bending at the pitcher's knees, a condition that should allow the pitcher's weight to sink or flex his legs for balance or thrust.

→ *Weight on inside of foot.* This term applies to either of the pitcher's feet. When either of his feet touches the ground, his weight should be placed on the inside of that foot, with the bulk of the ball of that foot as the focal point. Starting his push-off with his weight to the inside should provide the pitcher with better thrust and proper balance. Landing on the inside of his foot and keeping his weight there during and through the finish of his throw should create better angles and also help the pitcher maintain proper balance.

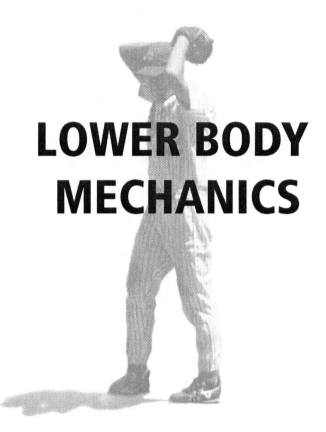

CHAPTER 1

LOWER BODY MECHANICS

DRILL #1: ISOLATED FEET

Objective: To improve a pitcher's throwing techniques. (In reality, however, with the pitcher's feet placed shoulder-width apart and kept in a stationary position, almost any phase of the throwing motion can be emphasized and improved by this drill.)

Description: Two or more players are required. Each player should have a partner. Each player takes a stance with his feet approximately shoulder-width apart and faces his partner with his feet parallel to his partner's shoulders. The throwing distance between the two partners may range from approximately 20 feet to as far as 90 feet. The distance will depend on the part of the throwing motion being emphasized. Special attention should be paid to weight distribution. As the ball is brought up and into throwing position, the pitcher's weight should shift to the inside part of his right foot (for a right-handed thrower). During the execution and following the release, the pitcher's weight should be shifted to the inside part of his left foot. In a sense, the pitcher is striding without taking a step. He is merely transferring his weight form his push-off foot to his stride foot. His feet should be stable.

This drill is designed to eliminate the stride. Since a major part of the pitcher's body movement is eliminated, it should be easier for the pitcher to attain and maintain his balance. As the pitcher throws, he should make sure his push-off knee stays inside his push-off foot and his stride knee stays inside his stride foot. Once this technique is per-fected, each player has developed an appropriate level of balance in throwing motion. He should be ready now to use this technique to improve other parts of his throwing motion. For example, the grip, the separation of hands, the height of the arm, the release of the ball, and the rotation of the ball can all be improved from this stationary stride position.

DRILL #2: THROWING ON ONE KNEE

Objective: To improve the ability of a pitcher to effectively transfer his weight from his back leg to his front leg; to work on keeping the stride knee inside the stride foot; to learn to keep the weight on the inside of the stride foot; to improve the right-to-left movement of the throwing arm action; to improve rotation and arm action; and to teach proper movement with the upper body.

Description: Each pitcher needs a partner. The pitchers should be divided into two lines, with the partners facing each other. Each pitcher drops to his push-off knee and assumes a stride position with his stride foot. Pitchers should begin throwing to each other at a distance of approximately 25 feet. As they are throwing to each other, careful attention should be paid to transferring the weight from inside the back knee to the inside portion of the stride foot. It is important that a pitcher maintain his balance throughout the weight transfer. Regardless of the skill being emphasized, proper balance and efficient weight transfer are necessary. If these two factors are not successfully achieved, no attempt should be undertaken to teach other movements with this drill. If such an attempt is made, the effort will be counterproductive. All factors considered, once the pitcher is able to throw from the on-one-knee position with good balance and is able to transfer his weight properly, many parts of his delivery will begin to show improvement.

DRILL #3: THROWING WITH BOTH KNEES ON THE GROUND

Objective: To improve both a pitcher's level of balance and his ability to properly transfer his weight during the throw; to develop the pitcher's ability to properly rotate the ball and achieve the desired arm angle when pitching; to improve the pitcher's ability to separate his hands in such a way to get his arms in a ready position to throw.

Description: The pitchers should be divided into two groups and positioned along two parallel lines. Each pitcher needs a partner. The partners face each other at a distance of approximately 25 feet. Each pitcher puts both knees on the ground parallel to his shoulders. The pitcher's knees should be approximately shoulder-width apart. The players begin the drill by playing catch, with the emphasis on having each player throw from the inside of his right knee to the inside of his left knee (a right-handed pitcher). During the drill, attention should continually be paid to having each pitcher maintain a proper degree of balance. An effort should be made to make sure each pitcher understands the routine. When balance and transfer of weight show progress, the throwing distance should be increased. As the distance increases, some pitchers may begin to have trouble with their balance. If problems arise, the distance between the players should be shortened and the pitchers directed to concentrate on shifting their weight from inside of their right knee to inside of their left knee. Pitchers should stay at the shorter distance until they are able to achieve both an appropriate level of balance and a sound weight transfer.

In time, and with a committed effort, each pitcher should be able to throw 90 feet and still adhere to the proper throwing techniques. The distance, of course, will be relative to the age group and the physical ability level of the individuals involved in the drill. From high-school age on up, 90 feet is a reasonable distance for testing both a pitcher's balance and his weight transfer.

DRILL #4: STATIONARY STRIDE DRILL

Objective: To provide the pitcher with an opportunity to work on specific aspects of his delivery; to improve balance.

Description: The drill involves having each pitcher place his stride foot in the desired position. The pitcher may then choose to concentrate on getting his throwing arm up and in a good position to throw. He may also find it important to concentrate on his chest, the position of his head, or the finishing position of his arm. This drill can have a positive impact on any of these movements. Each part or a combination of parts of the delivery can be emphasized with this drill. The pitcher begins the drill by making a simulated throw to a target. He simply keeps his feet in the desired position throughout the drill. In other words, he begins each action with his feet in a stationary stride position and completes the throwing motion with his feet in that same position. The initial focal point of the drill should be on balance. In that regard, the pitcher should work on transferring his weight from his push-off foot to his stride foot. The pitcher should pay close attention to how his weight is distributed on each foot. His weight should be placed on the ball of his push-off foot. During the push-off, his weight should shift to the ball of his stride foot. The proper transfer of weight is extremely important.

Once the pitcher has learned to shift his weight properly, he is ready to work from this position on other parts of his delivery. As the skill level of the pitcher progresses, it is extremely important to continue to maintain proper balance. If when moving to other segments of his delivery, the pitcher starts to lose his ability to properly maintain his balance, he should stop and go back to the weight-shift part of the drill. As in the isolated feet drill, it is important to remember the relationship of the knee to the foot. The push-off knee should be in front of the push-off foot, while the knee of the stride foot should be inside the stride foot. If the knee of the push-off foot gets outside the push-off foot, or if the knee of the stride foot gets outside the stride foot, the pitcher will lose his balance.

DRILL #5: BELLY BUTTON TO TARGET

Objective: To eliminate unnecessary movement; to provide a systematic and organized method of beginning the windup; to help the pitcher create better direction toward the target.

Description: This drill can be executed on either flat ground or the mound. While they are not mandatory, pitching rubbers would be very useful if they are available. Each pitcher should be equipped with a glove and a ball. The drill involves placing the pitchers in a line, or lines, facing the coach or designated leader. The lines should be short enough so the leader of the drill can easily see the participants. While one line is best, the drill can be effectively carried out with up to three lines. Lines of six players or fewer are ideal.

The drill begins by having each pitcher place both of his feet together with the toes or both feet pointing straight (i.e., toward the target). He then moves his left foot (right-handed pitcher) back so that the toe of that foot is even with the heel of his front foot. An effort should be made to ensure that the toes of both feet continue to point toward the target. The left foot should then be moved away from the right foot about six to eight inches, while keeping the toes pointed toward the target. At this stage of the drill, slight adjustments can be made with the spread of the feet. Some pitchers will be more comfortable and feel better balanced with a slightly wider spread, while others will feel more effective with a lesser spread. Extremes may create poor balance or even create a situation where the pitcher has poor alignment at the outset of his delivery.

It is important to establish the correct spacing of the pitcher's feet. The next step is to have each pitcher place all of his weight on his front foot. He will then be in a position with what is called a locked front knee. In order to shift his weight from that leg and get ready to place the foot on the rubber properly, he merely moves his weight to his back leg and locks his back knee. At this point, all of his weight is now on the ball of his back foot. Once his weight is on that foot, he is free to place his right foot on the rubber in either of two acceptable methods: a 45-degree angle or a parallel position. Regardless of the method employed, it is extremely important to keep the toe ahead of the heel at placement and during the push-off.

As his front foot is placed into the proper position, the pitcher's belly button should face the target. This stage is the beginning of the pitcher's windup. Even though work is being done with the belly button and the weight shift, it is important to coordinate the pitcher's hands with this maneuver. The pitcher will either lift his hands high or use a low-hands lift method. Terms that I prefer to use to describe this procedure with the hands are long strokers (high-hands lift) or short strokers (low-hands lift). When the pitcher gets to the top of his delivery, the action of his hands becomes his key to placing his foot properly on the rubber.

As the pitcher's hands are moved up to the top prior to placing his foot on the rubber, it is important for him to take his hands up, using the midline of his body as the guide. The midline of the body is important because that line keeps the hands directly in the center of his body and remains as a consistent line that never changes. Using this line also helps the pitcher keep a consistent pattern of movement.

This drill should be repeated until the pitcher can smoothly transfer his weight from one foot to the other, place his push-off foot on the rubber properly, keep his hands moving in a consistent pattern, and keep his belly button facing the target throughout the movement.

DRILL #6: BALANCE WITH PUSH-OFF FOOT

Objective: To practice and improve balance with the push-off foot; to help the pitcher develop a proper push-off position, as well as exert a higher level thrust.

Description: This drill can be started from either the windup or the stretch position. When he starts from the windup, the pitcher should place his push-off foot in the proper position. He should then lift his stride leg. When his leg gets to the top of the leg lift, the pitcher should hold that position for about three seconds. The pitcher's weight should be on the inside ball of the push-off foot. Prior to and during this holding pattern, the push-off foot should be stationary. The push-off foot should not move as the stride foot is lifted, and it should not move while the leg is in the holding pattern. The pitcher's push-off foot should be placed in a manner that sets his toe ahead of his heel. The toe should remain ahead of the heel during the leg lift and throughout the holding pattern.

When executed from the stretch, the drill involves having the pitcher merely lift his stride leg and hold for about three seconds once the front knee reaches the top of the leg lift. Working from the stretch position is easier for the pitcher because some extra movement has already been eliminated. For best results, both the stretch and the windup positions should be used when executing this drill.

Pitchers with good balance tend to adapt to this drill quickly. Those with poor balance often find this drill very difficult. Pitchers should practice this drill until they master it.

DRILL #7: BALANCE WITH THE STRIDE FOOT

Objective: To enhance the ability of the pitcher to establish balance on his stride foot; to help the pitcher learn to control his stride; ultimately, to enable the pitcher to create good angles toward the target.

Description: This drill can be done in a dry-run setting or can be practiced with actual throwing involved. From either setting, the pitcher should hold the stride position for about three seconds. It is important to keep in mind that proper balance and control of the foot are critical factors in sound pitching.

To execute the drill, the pitcher goes through the proper push-off and leg-lift portions of his delivery. He then either strides and simulates a throw, or he actually makes the throw if the drill is being done with live throwing. He should finish the action of the throwing arm, but hold his push-off foot in the air for about three seconds. The pitcher's weight should be on his stride foot, where he should maintain his balance. The weight of the pitcher should be placed on the inside ball of his stride foot. Once the stride foot makes contact with the ground, it should not move. It will not move if the pitcher has

proper balance. The pitcher's weight should remain on the inside part of his stride foot through his complete follow-through. The toe of his stride foot should be aligned toward the target and should be slightly inside the heel of his stride foot.

This holding pattern in the stride position for the prescribed time indicates the pitcher has learned to properly transfer his weight to his stride leg with control and balance. This action is also designed to enhance consistency with his release point and improve his ability to properly direct his foot toward the target.

DRILL #8: HOP FROM PUSH-OFF FOOT

Objective: To maintain balance and control of the push-off foot; to help the pitcher learn to place his push-off foot in the proper position and to keep his weight on the inside of his foot that has the toe aligned ahead of the heel.

Description: The drill is performed in a manner similar to Drill #6 (the balance with push-off foot). The drill begins with the pitcher balancing on his push-off foot. He then follows by taking three hop steps toward the target. On each hop step, he should place his push-off foot in the proper push-off-foot position. On each hop step, the push-off-foot toe should precede the heel of that foot. Furthermore, on each hop step, the pitcher's weight should be brought to the inside of and on the ball of his push-off foot. Careful attention should be paid to the pitcher maintaining proper control and balance of his body during each hop step. The pitcher should take low, controlled hop steps and concentrate on the proper placement of his foot on each step (i.e., he should take command of his push-off foot).

DRILL #9: HOP ON THE STRIDE FOOT

Objective: To enhance the ability of the pitcher to stride properly.

Description: This drill can be practiced from either the stretch position or a windup. The drill begins with the pitcher taking a stride and throwing or simulating a pitch. After striding, he takes three hop steps toward the target. The initial stride and the three-hop step strides should be executed with the pitcher's weight on the inside of his stride foot and the toe of the stride foot inside the heel of that foot and pointed toward the target. It is important for a pitcher to learn to control the stride foot. A good stride improves the pitcher's arm angle, his direction, and his balance.

Attention should be paid to the pitcher's weight distribution on each succeeding hop step. An effort should be made to ensure that the stride foot lands properly and maintains stability as the pitcher's weight is brought on it. In this instance, stability refers to the fact that the pitcher's foot does not swivel, roll, turn, or lose contact with the ground. It is important to emphasize to the pitcher that he should concentrate on the control and balance of his stride foot.

DRILL #10: HANG-HOP-HOP-HOP, THROW-HOP-HOP-HOP

Objective: To improve the pitcher's level of balance throughout his throwing motion; to enhance the pitcher's ability to maintain good balance at all times during both the push-off and the stride.

Description: This drill is a combination of the two preceding drills (Drills #8 and #9). The drill begins with the pitcher balancing on his push-off foot. He then takes three correct and controlled hop steps. On the third hop step, he throws or simulates a throw. He then completes the arm action of the throw and takes three hop steps on his stride foot. Again, these hop steps should be controlled and properly executed. The terminology for the drill is "hang-hop-hop-hop, throw-hop-hop-hop." The hops should be low, controlled, and well directed toward the target. If the pitcher loses control of his body or is unable to execute proper angles, he should stop engaging in the drill at that point. He should practice balancing on one foot at a time. Only when proper balance and control are achieved should he attempt the more complicated routine.

DRILL #11: LEG LIFT

Objective: To help the pitcher learn to control the height, direction, and movement of his stride leg.

Description: All factors considered, it is better (or perhaps easier) for the pitcher to begin this drill from the stretch position. However, he should eventually practice the drill from both the stretch position and the windup. From the stretch position, the pitcher lifts his stride leg up and toward the throwing-arm side of his body (i.e., an action that is also known as bringing the front knee toward the throwing-arm chin). This action should be repeated a number of times. The pitcher should then pause and look directly down the thigh of his stride leg when it is at the top of the lift. When the pitcher looks down his thigh and past his knee, he should be able to see the toe of the stride foot, and that toe should be hanging in a downward position. If the toe is in the proper position, it should not be extended or straightened too much, and should not be tucked under too far. Either extreme can be detrimental to the pitcher.

The leg lift is a controlled and relaxed maneuver that gets the pitcher ready to deliver the pitch to the plate. If the leg lift is too tight, the rest of the pitcher's body also tends to tighten up. If the pick-up leg is too straight or held out in front of the pitcher in an exaggerated manner, this motion tends to create overstriding or uncontrolled landings with the stride leg. An uncontrolled leg lift has a tendency to cause unrhythmic, uncontrolled, and unbalanced strides. Because the leg lift is an important part of the pitcher's delivery, this drill should be practiced on a regular basis.

DRILL #12: STRIDE-FOOT PLACEMENT

Objective: To practice and improve the correct placement of the pitcher's stride foot; to learn to control the stride foot.

Description: One or more pitchers can engage in this drill at the same time. A fence or support structure is needed to allow the pitcher to properly concentrate on his stride foot. The drill involves having each pitcher place his throwing hand on the top of a support structure. A short (four-foot) fence is ideal for the drill. A chair or other support structure may also be used. The pitcher simply needs an object to help him maintain his balance while he is involved with this particular drill. With his throwing hand giving him support, the pitcher assumes a stretch position with his feet. He then places his stride foot in front of his push-off foot. He lifts the heel of his stride foot, and with the toe of that foot contacting the ground, he traces the route that his toe takes from the top of the leg lift to the landing position (i.e., the pitcher is simply drawing a pattern with his lead-leg toe). The toe of his stride foot should not leave the ground and should stay completely closed until the last few inches of the pattern. To conclude the pattern, the toe opens enough to align the toe and the foot toward the target. Both the front knee and the bottom part of the leg remain closed. The entire foot does not open. Only the toe of the stride foot should control the slight opening of the foot. It should be kept in mind that the weight should transfer to the inside of his stride foot and remain inside that foot throughout the throw. It will usually take several tries for a pitcher to get the proper "feel" for this action.

Once the pitcher is able to place his stride foot in the proper position, he is ready to lift his stride leg and place it in the correct stride position. The drill then involves having the pitcher lift his stride foot off the ground and trace the pattern with his stride foot in the air. As he attains success at each level, he should raise his stride foot higher and continue to trace the desired movement patterns. The final phase of the drill involves having the pitcher raise his leg at the normal leg-lift position and, with his stride foot, follow the pattern that was originally traced on the ground. This sequence should be repeated several times until success is attained.

DRILL #13: STRIDE

Objective: To practice and improve the stride.

Description: The emphasis of this drill should be on controlling the position and direction of the stride leg and foot. It is important to establish a good base in order to throw with control and power. Weight distribution and balance are important to master. This drill is designed to enable the pitcher to concentrate on both respects. The drill begins by having the pitcher take a stride step. The pitcher should concentrate on contacting the ground with the inside ball of his foot. The stride knee should be bent and should remain bent as the pitcher's foot is placed at the stride spot. The transfer of the pitcher's weight to his stride foot is important. It should be transferred from the ball of the push-off foot to the ball of the stride foot. The toe of the stride foot should touch down first. The pitcher's weight should be shifted onto a balanced stride foot. The toe of the pitcher's stride foot shoe should point toward the target. In fact, it is best for most pitchers to align their front toes in a slightly pigeon-toed position. This action helps to keep the pitcher's weight on the inside part of the foot and also helps to keep the front knee closed. The pigeon-toed position, however, should not be exaggerated.

Some pitchers try to get their weight on the inside ball of the foot by raising the heel of that foot. The weight of these pitchers ends up on the toe of the foot rather than the ball of the foot. The entire stride foot should be in contact with the ground. The bulk of the pitcher's weight should transfer to the inside part of the foot. The ball of the foot should hold the weight. The weight should not be shifted to the heel and should not be allowed to drift to the outside part of the foot. The entire stride leg is important to the stride position. It should be under control both as it is lifted and as it is being planted and is taking on the weight transfer. The lead leg should direct, balance, and hold the pitcher's weight during both the release and the follow-through of each pitch. In order for a pitcher to maintain his balance and achieve a better angle for throwing, the lead-leg knee should remain bent throughout the pitcher's throwing motion. During and after the planting of the stride foot, the knee of the lead leg should be aligned inside the stride foot.

DRILL #14: WALKING STRIDE

Objective: To practice, concentrate on, and improve the pitcher's stride-foot position.

Description: One or more pitchers can take part in this drill at the same time. The pitchers involved in the drill form a line facing the coach. Ideally the line should consist of no more than six pitchers wide and two deep. Each pitcher assumes a stretch position. The drill begins by having each pitcher raise his lift leg a few inches and take a walking-stride step toward the target. Each pitcher then drags his push-off foot toward his stride foot. After touching the heel of his stride foot with his push-off foot, he should place it in a proper push-off position. Next, he lifts his stride leg slightly and takes another walking-stride step toward the target. The process is then repeated. As it is repeated, and as the pitcher begins to get the feel of striding properly, the stride leg can be lifted higher.

A great deal of attention should be paid to the proper planting of the stride foot. As this drill is repeated, it is important that each pitcher precisely apply the proper mechanics to the drill. It should be emphasized that the pitcher's weight should be placed on the inside of his stride foot. The stride foot should be placed down in a controlled manner. Although difficulties may occur anywhere in the process of striding, they more than likely will take place during the last six to 12 inches of the stride. The proper landing of the pitcher's stride foot should be emphasized. Often, minimal attention is paid to this vital part of the delivery. Every member of the pitching staff should be made to understand that a pitcher's stride is one of the keys to balance.

DRILL #15: HEEL OVER FROM A STATIONARY STRIDE POSITION

Objective: To help the pitcher learn the correct release and follow-through with his push-off foot.

Description: It is best to introduce this drill by simulating the throwing motion from a stationary stride stance. Each pitcher should be taught the proper techniques for striding before live throwing is added. The drill involves placing the pitchers in one or two lines facing the coach. The lines should be kept small enough so that each pitcher is in the sight line of the coach or group leader. As each pitcher simulates his throwing motion, the coach should watch the action of his push-off foot. During his entire throwing motion, the pitcher's feet should remain in the stationary stride position. As he starts to throw, his weight should be on the inside of his push-off foot. Meanwhile, the knee of his push-off leg starts moving downward and toward the target. This movement pushes the ball of his push-off foot back against the rubber. His push-off leg then begins to straighten and continues to drive toward the target. The ball of the pitcher's foot should remain in contact with the rubber.

At this point in the drill, under normal throwing conditions, the pitcher's push-off foot would release from the rubber, lift, and move in a circular motion to his throwing-arm side. During that circular motion, the heel of his push-off foot would start to turn over, and his foot would then continue the circle and contact the ground. It would complete the heel-over maneuver after contacting the ground. To simplify this drill and in order to make the maneuver easier to understand, the pitcher should not lift his push-off foot and form the circular motion to the throwing-arm side. Instead, he should merely make his throwing motion by keeping the ball of his push-off foot on the ground, and at the completion of his throw, turn his heel over. (Note: The lift and circle aspects will be incorporated into the next drill.)

This drill is designed to emphasize throwing and then turning the heel over. A common mistake by pitchers is to turn the heel over prematurely, a flaw that expends energy during the push-off and uses the power of the pitcher's back leg too soon. The purpose of the heel-over-at-finish is to allow the pitcher's arm to finish the throw. In other words, this action completes the pitcher's braking action and allows his arm to slow down naturally.

DRILL #16: PUSH-OFF KNEE

Objective: To help the pitcher keep his stride knee inside his stride foot; to help the pitcher bend his stride knee.

Description: The pitcher practices this drill from a stationary stride position. During a simulated throw, the pitcher drives his knee in a downward motion, touches that knee to the ground, and completes his throwing action. He finishes each simulated throw with his push-off knee on the ground and with his weight on the inside of his stride foot and with his stride knee inside his stride foot. The pitcher's throwing arm finishes on the outside of his stride leg with the elbow of his throwing arm touching the outside thigh of his stride leg.

The pitcher should repeat this action until he is able to perform the drill properly. He should keep in mind, however, that when he repeats this action, he may need to shorten his stride. If he does, it indicates to him that he was overstriding previously. This drill is designed to help the pitcher develop a better drive with his push-off leg. It also can help correct other parts of his delivery. This drill calls for the pitcher to exaggerate his move with his push-off knee. It should be noted, however, that his knee does not actually touch the ground during this normal push-off; it should merely drive in that direction.

DRILL #17: HEEL OVER WITH LIFT AND CIRCLE

Objective: To help the pitcher coordinate his push-off with the release and follow-through of his throw.

Description: The drill involves placing the pitchers in one or two lines facing the coach. The lines should be kept small enough so that each pitcher is in the coach's line of sight. The drill begins by having the pitcher simulate throws from the stationary stride position. As each pitcher simulates his throwing motion, attention should be paid to his push-off foot. On each simulated throw, the pitcher should start in the stationary stride position. Although his stride foot will remain in the same spot throughout his throwing motion, his push-off foot should release, pick up, and start to form a circle to the right (i.e., his pitching-arm) side. His push-off foot should continue forming a circle until it touches the ground. At this point, his foot finishes the circle, and that is the point where his heel should turn over.

The pitcher's weight should start on the ball of his push-off foot. His push-off knee should drive downward and toward the target. This action is designed to transfer his weight properly. The drive with his knee forces his push-off foot to drive back against the rubber. Next, his push-off leg straightens toward the target. At or near the release point, his push-off foot disengages from the rubber. At this point the pitcher should pick his foot up and start a circular motion outside his throwing-arm side. The circle should continue as his push-off foot lands. His pitching arm is now ready to finish the throw. The heel of his push-off foot then turns over and completes the circle. This action with his foot will allow his arm to fully complete his throwing motion. It should be kept in mind, however, that while the heel-over action begins as the pitcher's foot leaves the rubber, it should not be completed until after his foot has landed. This procedure should be repeated and an attempt made to connect the pieces. During his throw, the pitcher's body parts are releasing power. Each part of his throwing motion should be properly timed in order to make the entire motion effective. This drill is an effective way to accomplish that objective.

DRILL #18: CHAIR WITH THE HEEL OVER

Objective: To help the pitcher coordinate his heel-over motion with the finish of his arm action; to place the pitcher in a position to get the feel of throwing downhill.

Description: The pitchers are paired up. Each pitcher needs a chair for this drill. The drill involves having each pitcher place the inside part of his push-off foot on the chair seat. The chair should be placed on the throwing-arm side of the pitcher in the area where the foot would normally be at the top of the circle made by the pitcher's push-off foot during a normal throw. Room should be allowed on the seat for the foot to rotate over. The back of the chair is behind the foot. The stride foot should be placed in front of the chair at a normal stride length. The pitcher's stride foot should point to the target. From this position, each pair of pitchers will pitch to each other.

The pitcher throwing the ball begins the drill by shifting his weight to his push-off foot on the chair. During his throwing motion, the heel of his push-off foot is turned over, or rotated up and toward the throwing-arm side. This action represents the heel-over motion that should occur during a normal throw without the chair. Practicing with the pitcher's foot on the chair is designed to help in several ways. For example, it places the pitcher in a fixed position, which enables him to work on specific parts of his delivery with limited movement. In this particular drill, his push-off foot and stride foot are prepositioned. The heel-over motion can be practiced with the pitcher's foot already in the air and with his stride foot already placed correctly. This drill is designed to help the pitcher transfer his weight easily and control his stride properly.

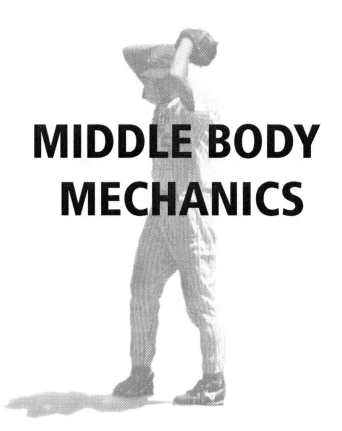

CHAPTER 2

MIDDLE BODY
MECHANICS

DRILL #19: LEG LIFT AND FRONT-HIP ELEVATION

Objective: To enhance the ability of the pitcher to coordinate his leg lift with his front hip, whereby his front hip is lifted higher than his back hip while maintaining a proper level of balance on his push-off foot.

Description: Similar to the Leg-Lift Drill (Drill #11), this drill is easier to perform from the stretch position. Accordingly, the pitcher should begin the drill from the stretch position and then progress to the windup when he is ready. This drill is similar to the Leg-Lift Drill, except that the emphasis is on the elevation of the pitcher's front hip. When the leg lift reaches its maximum height, the pitcher's front hip should be lifted so that is height is greater than the height of his back hip. This action should be done without having the pitcher lose his balance.

For the pitcher to maintain proper balance and move into a good thrust or push-off position, he should shift his weight to the inside part of his push-off foot. While doing this, he should make sure that his push-off leg starts in an unlocked position. When his weight is then shifted to his back (or push-off foot), that leg will flex or bend. The pitcher should pay close attention to his back knee as he elevates his leg and hip, making sure that his knee always precedes his push-off foot. In doing this, he enhances the ability of his back leg to provide thrust. Keeping the knee inside the foot will also push his weight down and against the inside part of his push-off foot.

Both this drill and the Leg-Lift Drill are extremely important. If the pitcher has a clear understanding of the purpose of both of these drills and has the ability to execute these drills correctly, the likelihood that he will be able to properly stride will be greatly enhanced.

DRILL #20: LEAD WITH THE HIP

Objective: To develop a good push-off by the pitcher in order to establish a sound stride.

Description: This drill is designed to help the pitcher to initiate his push-off with his front hip and to coordinate that move with the stride. This drill is an excellent way to introduce the elements of a proper stride to a relatively novice pitcher and show him how the stride should be started. The drill can also serve as a reminder and a viable means to make necessary adjustments for the more experienced pitcher. The pitcher begins the drill in the stretch position. Eventually, after the pitcher has mastered the stride from the stretch position, he progresses to the windup position. The pitcher starts the drill by lifting his front leg and elevating his front hip. His back knee should be unlocked and kept in front of his push-off foot. At this point, his front leg should be kept up as long as possible, while the pitcher simultaneously starts to move his front hip in a direction diagonally toward the stride spot. While practicing this move, the pitcher's weight should stay on the inside of his push-off foot as long as possible.

As the pitcher's front hip moves toward the stride spot, his front leg will eventually take over and finish the stride. If done properly, the movement with the hip supplies the beginning of the push-off. The pitcher's front hip should move a few inches (i.e., four frames on a stop-action, slow-motion video) before his front leg begins to move to stride. Most pitchers tend to be overactive with their stride legs. Overactivity with the stride leg and/or stride foot will negate some of the push-off and, in most cases, destroy the pitcher's balance.

The leg-lift, hip-elevation, bent-back knee, and hip-lead aspects of the drill should be practiced until the pitcher has control of these movements. It should be kept in mind that this sequence is the beginning of the stride and should be executed properly in order to achieve a sound stride. The pitcher's weight should be shifted to the inside part of his stride foot when the foot lands. Although it is not the primary emphasis of the drill, it should be noted that the leading of the hip is a very important part of the push and the stride.

DRILL #21: STRIDE FOOT IN THE CHUTE

Objective: To help the pitcher learn to consistently control the direction of his leg lift; to provide the pitcher with the opportunity to practice and master the beginning of his stride.

Description: This drill focuses on the position of the pitcher's stride foot and helps him to place that foot in the correct position consistently. The placement of the foot at leg lift helps the pitcher's push-off position and total body alignment. This drill is similar to the previous drill except that the pitcher needs a partner. The drill involves having one pitcher (i.e., the "active" pitcher) assume a stretch position, while his partner kneels on one knee and positions himself directly in front of the active pitcher. By lifting his stride leg repeatedly, the active pitcher eventually establishes the correct height of his stride leg and placement of the foot on that leg. The key for the pitcher is to bring his stride knee up and toward the throwing-arm side of his chin. He must also make sure that the angle of the knee is correct. If the pitcher encounters difficulty in establishing the correct leg lift and foot placement, a coach or observant partner may need to properly realign his stride foot and stride-leg lift.

Next, the drill involves having the kneeling pitcher form a chute with his hands at the spot at which the active pitcher should place his stride foot at the top of the leg lift. The active pitcher must be able to place the foot in the correct spot, or in the chute, at each leg lift before he moves on to the rest of the drill. The next part of the drill calls for the active pitcher to assume the correct starting position for the stride. The active pitcher then lifts his leg. In response, the kneeling pitcher then touches the active pitcher's stride foot when it is at the top of the leg lift. That hand should continue touching the foot until the foot leaves that area. The key to this part of the drill is to make sure the initial movement of the stride foot does not firmly push the kneeling pitcher's hand away. The active pitcher's hip should have started the stride, and his stride leg should have remained relaxed at the outset of the stride. If the front foot forcefully pushes against the kneeling pitcher's outstretched hand, it means the muscles of the active pitcher's leg have tightened too rapidly and the bottom part of the leg is taking over the stride. The result will often be a loss of balance and a poorly aligned throw with a premature push-off. This drill is designed to help each pitcher learn to control the position, direction, and movement of his leg lift and to properly execute the beginning of the stride. It also provides each partner with the opportunity to recognize and to teach the fundamentals and techniques for a properly executed leg lift and stride.

DRILL #22: LEADING WITH HIP, CHAIR

Objective: To improve the pitcher's leg lift and balance of his push-off foot; to enable the pitcher to get the feeling of leading with his front hip.

Description: A stable object (e.g., a chair, a fence, etc.) is needed as a benchmark for the pitcher's front foot. The drill begins by having the pitcher start from a stretch position. He should lift his front leg to its correct height and establish the distance that his stride foot is in at the top of the leg lift. Before proceeding with the remainder of the drill, it is important for the pitcher to place a chair at a distance that would allow his stride-foot toe to touch the edge of the back of the chair. As a guide, the throwing-arm side of the pitcher's chin should be used for the coiling position of the front foot. It should be emphasized to the pitcher that he should be able to look directly down his leg-lift thigh and see the toe of his stride foot. The chair should be placed in front of the pitcher, with those two markers as guides. If a fence or permanent object is used as a marker, the pitcher should adjust his position to the object.

As he performs the drill, the pitcher lifts his stride leg properly and gently touches the chair. Without allowing the chair to adjust the position of his foot, he merely holds his foot in a relaxed manner, with the toe pointing downward, and moves his front hip toward the stride spot. The objective of the drill is to control his stride foot and stride leg, while starting the push-off with his front hip. The chair (or fence) is merely a marker, or reminder, to make sure the pitcher's foot is extended and raised properly. The chair (or fence) enables each pitcher to see what he is doing with his front leg. The front leg should be relaxed, directed properly, and controlled.

DRILL #23: HAND SEPARATION AND BOTTOM OUT

Objective: To help improve the pitcher's ability to separate his hands consistently.

Description: This drill is designed to work on the direction in which the pitcher moves his hands and at what point he should begin to separate them as he moves them into the throwing position. The drill involves having each pitcher take his normal stride while simulating a throw. From this stationary stride position, he should place both hands together, as though operating from the stretch position. For the purposes of this drill, he should also hold his hands approximately waist high. The pitcher begins the drill by moving his hands up and down the front of his body, following the midline. The midline of the body is a very important guideline for the pitcher. By following this guideline, the pitcher will be better able to develop consistency with his hand movement and separation.

The next step in the drill is for the pitcher to move his hands upward a few inches as his hands follow the midline of his body. The pitcher then drops his hands downward through the midline. He lets his hands separate, but continues downward with both hands until they bottom out. As the pitcher drops his hands, he transfers his weight to the inside part of the push-off foot. He also makes sure that his hands and arms are relaxed throughout the maneuver. After bottoming out, his hands will automatically part from each other, or separate, and will begin to move in an upward arc.

The pitcher should keep in mind that a hard or forced action with his hands will prevent the natural movement described in this drill. Therefore, it is extremely important that the pitcher move his hands in a relaxed manner and allow the hand separation to be soft. Shortly after separating his hands, the pitcher's throwing hand will pass his push-off thigh with the back of his thumb facing that thigh. It is at this point that the pitcher should rotate the back of his thumb a quarter of a turn away from the thigh and continue to lift the ball into the throwing position with his fingers pointing toward the ground. During this motion, the pitcher should continue to raise his glove arm until it reaches the height of his chin so that the batter sees the back of his glove.

This drill should be repeated until the pitcher has become relaxed and consistent with the skills involved. The pitcher must be able to coordinate the shifting of his weight with the dropping and separation of his hands. He must also make sure that his hands separate at the same spot each time. While the point of separation will vary among pitchers, it should remain the same for each individual pitcher.

DRILL #24: THROWING-ARM LIFT

Objective: To teach the pitcher the proper technique in lifting his throwing arm; to help the pitcher keep his fingertips pointing toward the ground as he lifts the ball; to enable the pitcher to learn to control and guide his throwing arm into the correct position.

Description: While in the stationary stride position, the pitcher moves his hands up and down the midline of his body. As he brings his hands down and separates them, the pitcher shifts his weight to the inside part of his push-off foot. In this drill, the pitcher rotates the back of his throwing-hand thumb a quarter-turn away from the thigh of his push-off leg. He also allows his throwing arm to swing back and upward. As the pitcher reaches back and lifts his arm into the throwing position, he makes sure that his fingertips remain pointed toward the ground throughout. Meanwhile, his throwing hand should reach its maximum height while above his head. As he lifts his arm, the pitcher should ensure a functional and ready throwing position by bending his throwing-arm elbow. When the hand above his head reaches its maximum height, the pitcher's weight should already be transferred to the inside of his push-off foot.

Close attention should be paid to the rotation of the pitcher's throwing hand after separation and how that hand is taken back and lifted. By rotating the ball a quarter of a turn away from the thigh, the pitcher will prevent his throwing arm from wrapping.

This drill should be repeated until the pitcher has mastered it. This drill is a good exercise to use with both the inexperienced and the experienced pitcher. Not only can it help an inexperienced pitcher develop proper lifting procedures, it can also enable an experienced pitcher to practice and maintain sound techniques.

DRILL #25: ARM LIFT WITH BATTING "T"

Objective: To practice getting a pitcher's throwing arm into the proper position—particularly the arm-lift phase of the pitching delivery.

Description: Two pitchers will share a batting "T". One pitcher acts as a feeder and places the ball on the "T". The other pitcher, the active pitcher, uses the "T" as a learning tool. After placing the "T" at the spot where his arm lift begins, the active pitcher assumes the stationary stride position. He starts the drill by shifting his weight to the inside of his back foot. He then reaches back and picks the ball up off the "T" and throws it to the target, either a catcher or another pitcher. When he takes the ball off the "T", his fingertips should point toward the ground. As he lifts his arm to the top of the throwing position, his fingertips remain in that downward position. In other words, he is taking the ball off the "T" by gripping the ball from the top and lifting straight up from the top of the "T". During his throwing action, the pitcher should pay attention to how he is lifting his arm and transferring his weight from one foot to the other. This weight transfer should be achieved as it was explained in the Stationary Stride Throwing Drill (Drill #4). The major purpose of this drill, however, is to improve the ability of the pitcher to perform the arm lift properly. When the pitcher can successfully execute the proper arm lift from the "T," he should remove the "T" and make a few throws from the stationary stride position. If he continues to lift his arm properly, he no longer needs the "T".

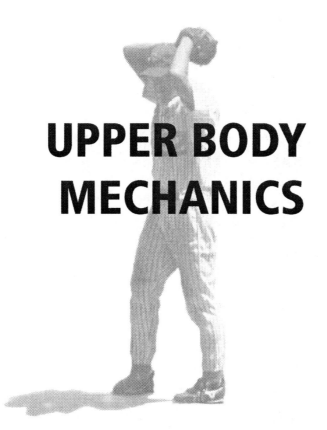

CHAPTER 3

UPPER BODY
MECHANICS

DRILL #26: TRAJECTORY

Objective: To help the pitcher establish and maintain the proper throwing angle; to teach the pitcher how to get his fingers on top of the ball.

Description: This drill is designed not only to help the pitcher develop the feel of throwing downhill, but also to help the pitcher correct flaws in the routing of his throwing arm. The pitcher starts the drill in the stationary stride position, with his throwing arm held at the top of the throwing motion. He then begins his live or simulated throw. At the outset of the drill, the pitcher displays a bent, or forward, wrist. As he continues his throwing motion, however, his wrist will bend backward, thus initiating the wrist-snap action that is completed at the finish of the arm extension.

What makes this drill particularly effective is that it calls for the pitcher to begin with his arm already at the desired height. As a result he does not have to worry about separating his hands and lifting his arm. This drill also enables the pitcher to engage in simulated and short-distance throwing that can help him develop a downward and extended motion. This drill should be practiced regularly, until the height of the pitcher's throwing hand during a regular throw matches the height of the throwing hand called for in this drill.

DRILL #27: FRONT ARM

Objective: To help the pitcher properly direct and control the movement of his front arm.

Description: The pitcher performs this drill from the stationary stride position and begins at the point at which his hands separate. At the point of hand separation, the pitcher's glove hand continues to drop and begins to move in an arc toward the target. As he proceeds, the pitcher should take his front arm toward the target with the back of his glove facing the hitter. At the same time, he should control the height of the lift of his front arm by stopping it at chin level. With his entire body now in a closed position, the pitcher must open up the top half of his body to complete the throw. He can help accomplish that by turning the thumb of his glove hand over. Next, the pitcher should lift the heel of his glove hand and then follow by bringing his elbow back in and brushing it against his rib cage. As such, the drill consists of the following steps: (1) take the arm toward the target, (2) lift the glove to chin level, (3) turn the thumb over, (4) raise the heel of the hand, and (5) bring the elbow in and brush it against the rib cage.

The pitcher should remember that the speed of his front arm should be controlled by the speed of his throwing arm. In other words, if the throw is easy and rather slow, the front arm should be rather slow. On the other hand, if the throw is fast, the front arm should also be fast. A rhythmical throw is one that exhibits good coordination between the front arm and the throwing arm. The pitcher should practice this drill until the techniques involved in executing a sound front-arm action become a habit.

DRILL #28: CHEST TO TARGET

Objective: To encourage the pitcher to throw his chest at the target so that he develops a barrel chest when delivering the baseball.

Description: This drill is designed to emphasize the need for the pitcher to keep his breasts parallel to the ground. Level breasts and a barrel chest create better body angles and provide greater extension of the pitcher's arm toward the target. As such, this drill can help the pitcher create a longer lever for throwing. This drill can either be done in a dry-run setting or with live throwing. In a dry-run setting, the pitcher or pitchers should stand in a line facing the instructor. With live throwing, the pitchers should split up into pairs and form two parallel lines. The drill involves having each pitcher assume the stationary stride position. As the pitcher throws, or simulates a throw, he should first emphasize keeping his breasts parallel to the ground. At the same time, the pitching coach should pay close attention and should emphasize to the pitcher the importance of keeping his chest level. If his front arm drops too low or his head tilts to the side, the pitcher's breasts will not stay level.

Once he has mastered the first part of the drill, the pitcher should concentrate on extending his level chest toward the target. The coach should help by telling the pitcher, "Throw the breasts to the target," or "Reach out and try to touch the target with your chest." If the pitcher's chest is extended properly, his head will finish well in front of his front knee. After he has completed his throwing action, the pitcher should evaluate his body angles while throwing. His chest and head should be aligned toward the target at the completion of each throw. As the pitcher begins to extend his chest, he should arch his back. This arching will help him extend his chest to the target. With proper extension and a level chest, the pitcher will notice that he is able to gain distance on his arm extension.

As this drill is conducted, other mechanical flaws in the pitcher's delivery may become apparent. For example, incorrect positioning of the pitcher's head, improper movement of his front arm, or other flaws may prevent the pitcher from creating a level, extended chest. If so, these flaws may need to be addressed before moving on to other drills or issues. As such, this drill should receive a lot of repetitions in practice and should receive the close attention of both the pitcher and the pitching coach when it is performed.

DRILL #29: CHIN UP

Objective: To enhance the ability of the pitcher to properly align his chin toward the target.

Description: By directing his chin to the target and making sure the bottom of his chin is parallel to the ground, the pitcher will be able to achieve greater extension to the target with the top part of his body. This drill is closely related to the Chest-to-Target Drill (#23). It is designed to reinforce the point that proper work with the chin will help the chest and vice versa. This drill can be done effectively in either a dry-run or a live setting. In a dry-run setting, the pitchers will form one or two lines. For best results, no more than six pitchers should be permitted in each line. If the pitchers are actually throwing, they should be divided into pairs and then assume the stationary stride position. The drill can also be practiced during a bullpen workout, wherein the same fundamentals apply.

Many pitchers tend to pull their chins down toward their chests as they throw. Others tilt, or pull, their chins to the side. As such, it is important that every pitcher keeps in mind that either of these actions can throw him out of proper alignment and cause him to throw with a concave chest. By keeping his chin up and taking his chin to the target, the pitcher can help maximize his total delivery.

Although the angle of the chin is just one of many facets of the pitcher's delivery, it is equally as important as any of the other mechanical aspects. Proper alignment of the chin will help proper alignment of other parts of the body. Accordingly, the pitcher can reap major benefits if he makes a concerted effort to master the techniques involved in this drill.

DRILL #30: EYES TO THE TARGET

Objective: To improve the ability of the pitcher to direct his eyes at the target.

Description: The ability to direct his eyes properly is important to a pitcher because if his eyes are level, parallel to the ground, and directed at the target, the rest of his body will follow and create better angles, as well as improve his balance. This drill can be performed by either simulating the throw or actually throwing the ball. If the pitcher needs to correct a major flaw, however, the dry-run setting will probably be more effective. Of course, the final test will involve live throwing activities. For dry-run drill purposes, one or two lines of pitchers are required. Each line should be no more than six players wide. The drill involves having each pitcher assume the stationary stride stance and face the pitching coach. Each pitcher's role in the drill is to keep his eyes level and throw them directly toward the target as he makes or simulates each throw. The pitcher should repeat this drill and continue practicing it even after he notices progress. This drill may also help the pitcher properly align his chest. If used correctly, the drill can also help ensure that the pitcher's chin is also properly aligned. Incidentally, this drill is closely related to the two previous drills (#28 and #29). It can also be very effective when utilized in conjunction with live bullpen drills. Finally, adherence to the principles and techniques involved in this drill has been shown to have a positive impact on a pitcher's level of control.

DRILL #31: CHEST TO THIGH

Objective: To improve the ability of the pitcher to properly follow through.

Description: It should be noted that this drill should be performed only after the pitcher has mastered the three previous drills (#29-#31). The drill begins by having the pitcher extend his chest to the target and release the ball. The pitcher should make sure his arm finishes by touching the outside of his stride leg. Meanwhile, the bottom of his chest should squeeze against the thigh of his stride leg. With regard to effective pitching mechanics, the term "bend the back" is often used. To follow-through properly and truly finish the throwing motion, the pitcher needs to bend his back. He can only accomplish this, however, after extending his chest, head, and arm toward the target. By touching his chest to his thigh, the pitcher should find it easier to finish his throwing motion. Initially, the pitcher should practice this drill from a stationary stride stance and should simulate the throwing motion. He can then advance to live throwing as his skill level improves. The key is for the pitcher to make this action part of his competitive throwing motion. Those pitchers who find it difficult to adhere to the proper techniques for following through when throwing live should go back to the stationary stride position and continue at that position until they fully grasp the concept.

DRILL #32: RIGHT TO LEFT (RIGHT-HANDED PITCHERS)

Objective: To ensure that the pitcher, at the end of each throw, extends his arm toward the target and finishes with his right elbow touching the outer thigh of his stride leg; to help improve the ability of the pitcher's hand and wrist to finish in a relaxed position.

Description: It should be noted that the proper follow-through will result in a natural braking process of the pitcher's throwing arm, while an incorrect follow-through indicates that the pitcher is straining his arm or some other body part. The drill can be performed in either a dry-run setting or live action. In a dry-run setting (done from a stationary stride stance), the drill is designed to help the pitcher develop the feel of proper arm action. As he simulates the throw, he should make sure the other parts of the throwing motion are done correctly. He should be particularly concerned with getting good arm, chest, and head extension before he touches his elbow to the outside of his thigh. Once the pitcher has "thrown" correctly in the simulated throwing phase of the drill, the next step in the drill is to have the pitcher follow the same procedure during live throwing. The live throwing phase of the drill should also start from the stationary stride position and should progress to both the stretch and the windup positions. The pitcher should throw at a controlled speed until he achieves the desired results. Once the pitcher feels comfortable with his arm extension, he should increase his throwing speed. At the same time, he should also make sure that his right-to-left action is correct. Obviously, the final test of the pitcher's ability to properly follow through is the game. As such, the pitcher should keep practicing the right-to-left action in drills until he can include the maneuver in his normal throwing motion during actual competition.

DRILL #33: CHEST TO THIGH WITH A TENNIS BALL

Objective: To improve the ability of the pitcher to properly follow through with each throw so that he can minimize the strain on his arm and allow other body parts to assist his arm in the throw.

Description: This drill is the same exercise as the previous drill (#32), with the exception of incorporating a tennis ball. In this drill, the pitcher should extend his chest to the target and should finish by squeezing the tennis ball. The tennis ball acts as a reminder to the pitcher. In order to squeeze the tennis ball, the pitcher must bend his back and must exert enough force to complete the task. The addition of the tennis ball to the drill is only for those pitchers who have difficulty with the final phase of the follow-through. As such, they may need the extra piece of equipment to give them a specific focal point. A squeaking doll is an even better tool for those who need both sound and feel as a reminder.

For any pitcher who is having difficulty with this part of his delivery, it is best to simulate the motion from the stationary stride position. As the pitcher begins to grasp the concept and progresses to the point where he is consistent with his delivery, he should advance to live throwing. He should also repeat the drill a few minutes each day until he has mastered it. This drill can also be executed from the stretch position and the windup position. Furthermore, it can also be used as part of a bullpen workout.

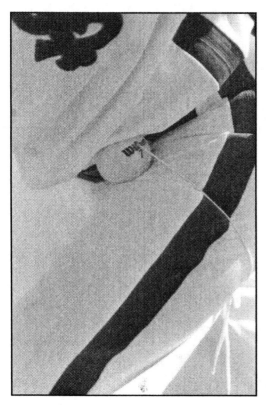 

DRILL #34: BROOMSTICK

Objective: To help the pitcher who has difficulty getting his arm high enough to throw in a downward angle.

Description: As such, this drill is designed to help the pitcher get his arm at the proper height above his head by the time the foot lands in a stride position. The drill is important because often a pitcher will drop his elbow too low or get his fingers under the ball. Either mistake will cause him to throw too high and also have an adverse effect on his breaking pitches. The pitcher who has these flaws may eventually suffer an arm injury. If he does this drill correctly, the pitcher will improve his curveball and create a more consistent and functional release point on all of his other pitches as well.

This drill is best done in the bullpen. A broomstick or even a bat can be used as a teaching aid. While the pitcher is throwing to the catcher from the pitching rubber, he should use the broomstick as a visual hurdle that his throwing hand must throw over. The pitching coach should stand to the side and in front of the pitcher, about 15 to 20 feet away from the pitcher and to the throwing-arm side of him so that the broomstick can be held horizontally in front of the pitcher. The coach should then raise the broomstick to a height that challenges the pitcher to raise his arm sufficiently to throw the ball on a downward angle to the target. As the pitcher starts to release the pitch, the coach should lower the broomstick for safety reasons.

When using this drill to improve the rotation and angle of his curveball, the pitcher should find it challenging to get his throwing hand at the proper height while he is imagining that he is extending his arm and reaching over the broomstick. At the end of the pitcher's arm extension, his middle finger should rush over the top of the baseball and pull down on the front of the ball. As the pitcher tries to meet the challenge, his hand and arm should be moving in the proper direction. On the curveball, his throwing hand should pass by and over the bill of his cap on the throwing-arm side and gain extension toward the target by then passing over the opposite side of the cap's bill. Although the ball is not actually released at that spot, the pitcher should get the feeling that it is released there. A baseball bat can be substituted for the broomstick in the drill, although the broomstick is lighter and easier to raise and lower.

DRILL #35: MAT TO HELP ARM ANGLE

Objective: To improve the ability of the pitcher who drags his arm through the delivery to adhere to the proper arm angle when throwing. (Note: Such a dragging of the arm will cause the pitcher to struggle with his trajectory.)

Description: The drill involves placing a piece of rubber conveyor belt or firm rubber mat on the ground in front of the pitcher and directly in line with the target. The mat should be at least eight feet long and two feet wide. Thirty-five feet should be marked off from the rubber or from the push-off foot. Place the mat lengthwise between the pitcher and the catcher. The drill can be done on flat ground: For best results, however, the pitching mound should be used. The drill also involves a catcher in full gear who should be stationed in his normal position behind home plate. A like distance is necessary if the drill takes place on flat ground. It is also necessary that the pitcher be warmed up and ready to throw at his normal speed before the drill begins.

The pitcher's task is to throw each pitch by hitting the mat first before arriving at the target. In other words, he is making a one-hop throw to the catcher. To get consistent results, the pitcher's hand should be higher than his head by the time his stride foot lands. After one or two attempts, he should be aware of a noticeable difference in his arm angle. The pitcher should continue with this part of the drill until he has mastered the skills involved. Next, the pitcher should throw two pitches using the hop method and two pitches directly to the catcher. The two pitches thrown without the hop should be low pitches directed at the imaginary hitter's knees.

The pitcher should continue to alternate his throws in this fashion. After eight or 10 pitches, he should begin to make fewer one-hop throws and more direct throws at the hitter's knees. By using a ratio of five direct throws to every one hop throw, the pitcher should be able to slowly wean himself from the mat. It should be noted that even though the pitcher should notice positive results after his first attempt at performing this drill, he may require more than one session to fully master the desired techniques.

DRILL #36: RELEASE POINT

Objective: To improve the ability of the pitcher to maintain a consistent release point—a factor that will improve his body alignment toward the target and result in better control, greater velocity, and better stuff.

Description: For this drill, a screen and some sort of target are employed. While a protective screen will be adequate for this drill, it should be at least four-feet wide and eight feet tall and heavy enough to stop a ball traveling approximately 20 feet. The screen should be placed approximately 20 feet in front of the pitcher, who is stationed atop the mound on a pitching rubber. The screen should be centered with an imaginary line drawn from the mound to home plate.

Directly on the imaginary line and behind the screen, an adjustable release-point stand should be positioned. Typically, such a stand is made from a plow disc and two small pipes. One of the pipes is welded to the disc, while the other fits inside the welded pipe. Nail-size holes are drilled in both pipes so that the inside pipe can be moved up and down with a nail holding it at the desired height. On the sliding pipe, a small goal post is welded. The small goal post is made of a small-diameter, 12-inch pipe with an eight-inch pipe welded to each end of the 12-inch pipe. The small goal post is centered and welded to the adjustable pipe. The drill involves adjusting the middle of the goal post to the height that represents the desired release point for the pitcher who is preparing to take part in the drill.

The pitcher should work on his release point by throwing to an imaginary catcher behind home plate. The screen will stop the pitch and allow the pitcher to retrieve the ball quickly, as well as allow him to drill alone if necessary. While throwing at the target, he should try to release the ball between the two small pipes representing the release point. As the ball is released, the pitcher's throwing hand should continue on a path that causes it to pass through the path leading to the middle of the small goal post.

DRILL #37: FUNNEL

Objective: To help the pitcher develop correct angles toward the target so that he improves his push-off, and the angle and direction of the arm will improve the release point.

Description: This drill is literally designed to help the three most important factors of the pitcher's delivery: balance, thrust, and angles. This drill can be done two different ways (from the windup and stretch positions) and on two different types of surfaces (either flat ground or the pitching mound). All factors considered, the pitching mound is the best setting because of the mound's slope.

For the pitcher with a fairly good sense of imagination, this drill should help his delivery. The drill involves having the pitcher imagine that a large funnel is directly in front of the pitching mound, just beyond his stride, with the open mouth of the funnel facing him and the small spout directed at the catcher. As the pitcher throws the pitch, he should make a mental picture of every part of the throwing motion, gathering up the pitching hand and helping it move forcefully and easily through the spout of the funnel. Furthermore, he should attempt to direct each body part toward the funnel spout. During this drill, the pitcher should try to correct any flaw in his stride that prevents the stride from being directed toward the target. If his front arm, for example, slings open too quickly, he should correct that flaw. In other words, his every movement should be directed to the funnel spout. No detours whatsoever should be acceptable.

Another way the pitcher can perform this drill is to draw the letter V in the dirt in front of his stride foot. The wide part of the letter V should face the pitcher, while the point of the V should be directed at the target. Thus, the letter V represents the imaginary funnel. It may be better for some pitchers to use the V because, in this instance, the funnel is actually visible to them. The V, or funnel, can even be drawn in the dirt during competition. When he uses the V, the pitcher should stride directly toward the point of the V. While he should pitch by throwing toward the open part of the V, at the same time he should direct his throwing motion through the point of the V.

CHAPTER 4

IMPROVING VELOCITY

DRILL #38: AIR IT OUT

Objective: To improve the level of speed on the pitcher's fastball, as well as his overall level of arm strength and power.

Description: This drill is designed not only to help develop a pitcher's arm strength and arm speed, but also to enhance the ability of the pitcher to adjust his speeds without a drastic change in his mechanics. On the other hand, anytime hard throwing is mentioned, warning flags go up. Perhaps they should, but the simple truth is that if he does not throw hard, the pitcher cannot maintain or improve his throwing power or throwing speed. No matter the exercise, it must be combined with hard throwing if the pitcher's goal is to maximize the sheer speed of his fastball. In reality, pitchers can and should throw with maximum effort. They should not do this on every pitch, however. Before throwing at maximum exertion, the pitcher should be in good shape and should be properly warmed up to throw. He should also be mechanically sound before attempting maximum-effort throws.

Most coaches have heard the saying, "If you don't use it, you will lose it." That statement is particularly true of the throwing fastball. Throwing hard requires effort. Like a sprinter in track and field, the fastball pitcher needs to use his ability to the fullest in order to maintain or surpass his best mark. This statement is not to say that every sprint or every pitch calls for an individual's ultimate effort. A sprinter, for example, may choose to expend a maximum effort while sprinting only once or twice a week, while allowing for recovery time between such efforts. By the same token, a pitcher could adopt a similar philosophy. For example, a pitcher's maximum effort should involve 10 to 15 pitches at the end of each regular bullpen workout; the rest of the pitches thrown in those regular bullpen workouts should be thrown at his working speed or less. His working speed is usually about three to six miles per hour slower than his maximum speed. During intrasquad games, the pitcher should throw about 10 percent of his total number of pitches with a maximum-speed effort. He should be selective, however, and should make sure that when he selects a maximum-effort pitch, it does not work to his disadvantage. For example, he might wait for a 0-2 count or a 1-2 count or any other count that would not cause him to put himself in a jam. As such, in a 30-pitch outing, only three pitches of this type need to be thrown. As such, in a 100-pitch outing, only 10 need to be thrown. In reality, this approach could even work to the advantage of the pitcher. For example, a pitch thrown three to six miles per hour faster than the normal pitches the hitter usually sees could create a timing problem for that hitter.

DRILL #39: STRAIGHT-LINE LONG TOSS

Objective: To improve the ability of the pitcher to get good rotation on the ball; to enhance the pitcher's level of balance; to improve the pitcher's level of thrust; to enhance the pitcher's level of correct angles; to improve the pitcher's level of throwing-arm strength.

Description: The pitchers should pair up and begin warming up by playing catch. Only after each pitcher's arm is ready to throw at game speed can the drill commence. The initial step in the drill involves determining the straight-line throwing mark for each pitcher. To do this, the drill should start with the pitchers 60 feet apart. At this distance, the pitcher's goal should be to make a throw that does not have an arc. If the pitcher cannot throw a straight-line throw at this distance, he should reduce the distance until he can make such a throw. Accordingly, whatever maximum distance the pitcher can throw without making an arc becomes his straight-line throwing mark. If the pitcher can successfully make a non-arc throw at 60 feet, he should increase the distance until the throw develops an arc. Once again, the distance of the pitcher's longest throw without an arc becomes his straight-line throwing mark. Each time this drill is conducted, the pitcher should try to improve on his mark. The straight-line throwing portion should take no more than 10 throws. In fact, 10 throws should be the maximum. For maintenance purposes, five to 10 throws are adequate. For building (i.e., developmental) purposes, eight to 10 throws should be made.

It is important that both the coach and the pitcher strictly adhere to several cautionary guidelines concerning this drill. For example, any pitcher who performs this drill should be fully warmed up, be in good shape, and have good pitching mechanics. Furthermore, he should stop throwing if he experiences any pain. In other words, both the pitcher and the coach must be serious about doing things correctly and must be prudent enough to understand the importance of proper conditioning and throwing readiness.

Pitchers should keep in mind that results will only come from hard work, commitment, and consistency. As such, to expect a noticeable gain, the pitcher should do this drill at least twice a week for at least a month. The drill can be done more than twice a week if the pitcher's other activities during the week are light.

DRILL #40: RADAR GUN

Objective: To help the pitcher learn to vary the speed of his pitches through the use of a radar.

Description: Each pitcher should know his working speed. Unless he is a pitcher with an overpowering fastball, he should vary the speed of his fastball. By practicing regularly with the radar gun, the pitcher can learn how to estimate his throwing speed and then can decide how to utilize different kinds of fastballs. The difference in the speed of a fastball and a change-up, or a fastball and a curveball, can be measured with the radar gun. As the pitcher makes use of the radar gun on a daily basis, he should learn that the difference of three to four miles per hour in a pitch is relatively easy to achieve—and it can be done without a noticeable difference in the mechanics of his arm action. The pitcher should establish his working speed by determining the maximum speed at which he can maintain control. Next, he should learn to throw the fastball at different speeds within a range of four to five miles per hour of his working speed. His working speed will be a few miles per hour less than his maximum speed. This familiarity with changing speeds on his fastball will help the pitcher develop proper variations of speed between his fastball and his curveball. Both his curveball and his change-up should be about 10 to 12 miles per hour slower than his fastball.

RADAR GUN CHART

Name:_____Date:_____

FB CU CH SL Other Pitches	FB CU CH SL Other Pitches	FB CU CH SL Other Pitches
1	19	37
2	20	38
3	21	39
4	22	40
5	23	41
6	24	42
7	25	43
8	26	44
9	27	45
10	28	46
11	29	47
12	30	48
13	31	49
14	32	50
15	33	51
16	34	52
17	35	53
18	36	54

FB	CU	CH	SL	Other Pitches		FB	CU	CH	SL	Other Pitches		FB	CU	CH	SL	Other Pitches
55						87						119				
56						88						120				
57						89						121				
58						90						122				
59						91						123				
60						92						124				
61						93						125				
62						94						126				
63						95						127				
64						96						128				
65						97						129				
66						98						130				
67						99						131				
68						100						132				
69						101						133				
70						102						134				
71						103						135				
72						104						136				
73						105						137				
74						106						138				
75						107						139				
76						108						140				
77						109						141				
78						110						142				
79						111						143				
80						112						144				
81						113						145				
82						114						144				
83						115						145				
84						116						146				
85						117						147				
86						118						150				

SUMMARY: DID I VARY SPEEDS WELL?

Best Speed	Workable Speed
FB _____	FB _____
CU _____	CU _____
CH _____	CH _____
SL _____	SL _____

Range

FB _____	FB _____
CH _____	CH _____

CHAPTER 5

IMPROVING CONTROL

DRILL #41: BODY TARGET

Objective: To help the pitcher develop better control.

Description: Prior to the drill, the pitchers pair up and begin playing catch at a distance of approximately 30 feet. As their arms get loose, the pitchers move farther away from each other, to a distance of approximately 60 feet, 6 inches. This drill calls for each pitcher to make five throws to each of six targets. The target for the first five throws is the right shoulder of the pitcher's partner. The second target is the right hip of the partner. The third target is the right knee. The fourth target is the left shoulder. The fifth target is the left hip. The sixth target is the left knee. When each pitcher has finished, he has made 30 throws at six different targets. While he is throwing, however, the pitcher needs to visualize the target, commit to hitting that target, and then execute his plan.

It is important for the pitcher to visualize quickly and clearly. Intent is equally important. He must trust his arm to execute the task, learn to block out distractions, and see only the target. In other words, the pitcher should let his arm do what his mind visualizes. It is important that the pitcher should practice this drill every day in warm-ups. In fact, this drill can be done every time the pitcher plays catch.

DRILL #42: TARGET THROWING WITH TIRES

Objective: To help the pitcher develop better control; to help the pitcher develop the skill and technique to hit his target.

Description: This drill requires an automobile tire, which can be tied to a protective screen, propped against the screen, or tied to a rope, allowing the tire to hang. The pitcher may perform this drill on flat ground or from the pitching rubber. He does not necessarily need to throw at full speed, however, because a pitcher with good control has control of his pitches at various speeds.

In this drill, the pitcher's objective is to throw the ball through the opening in the tire. Of course, the tire can and should be moved to various spots, representing different parts of the strike zone. The pitcher should keep in mind that the tire is simply the target. The tire is big enough to be noticed. Furthermore, the small opening in the middle of the tire offers a reasonable challenge to the pitcher. It is important to remember that throwing to a definite target is always more productive than just playing catch.

DRILL #43: ISOMETRICS AND GRIP

Objective: To help strengthen the pitcher's fingers; to improve the ability of the pitcher to "feel" the baseball.

Description: The drill enables a pitcher to strengthen his hand and fingers by doing isometric exercises with the baseball. The pitcher should hold the ball with a fastball grip and then squeeze for a few seconds. He should repeat this process a few times each day. Next, the pitcher should use the curveball grip and squeeze the baseball for a few seconds. He should repeat this process a few times each day as well.

The pitcher should also use a curveball grip and spin the ball in the air. As he grips the ball, he should try to apply maximum pressure with his middle finger and see how much help comes from his thumb.

A pitcher should become as familiar as possible with the various grips of the baseball as well as the action of the ball. He should develop finger and hand strength. The pitcher should also keep in mind that if he is to have good control and good stuff, he must develop a "feel" for the ball.

DRILL #44: THROWING TO A STRING TARGET

Objective: To enhance the pitcher's level of control.

Description: The drill involves taking two strong pieces of string and tying one end of each to a standard. One end is tied at the top of the standard, while the other is attached at the bottom of the same pole. Because the distance between the top and bottom strings should be equal to the height of an average strike zone, the first string should be placed at knee height and the other string should be tied approximately at armpit height. Next, both strings should be run horizontally to another standard and tied to it. The standards should be about eight feet apart, a distance that is designed to make the drill safer and more functional for the catcher.

After tying the two horizontal strings, the two strings that represent the inside edge and the outside edge of the strike zone are ready to be connected. The coach should go to the middle of each horizontal string, measure eight and a half inches in each direction, and mark each spot. The next step for the coach should be to tie two perpendicular strings to the horizontal strings and connect them at the marked spots. With the strings connected and placed directly over home plate, the pitcher should be able to see both the width and height of the zone (17 inches wide and approximately 26 inches high). This drill can either consist of a few concentrated throws or can comprise an entire bullpen workout.

DRILL #45: EXAGGERATED TARGET

Objective: To help those pitchers who are "psychologically bothered" by home plate.

Description: This drill is designed for those pitchers who essentially place too much importance on home plate and thus tend to become extremely wild. The harder they try, the more frustration they seem to experience. This drill attempts to make home plate an insignificant factor by having the pitcher simply throw to the catcher. The catcher should set up in exaggerated spots. For example, he may take a position behind home plate but also move a good distance to either side of the plate. In a sense, the catcher is saying, "Come on, pitcher, forget about the strike zone and just hit my mitt." Success is simply measured by whether or not the pitcher can play catch with the catcher. As the drill progresses, the catcher should continue to station himself in extremes, away from the strike zone. When the pitcher becomes more relaxed and is able to hit the catcher's mitt, the catcher should begin to place himself closer to the strike zone at each succeeding change of position. Eventually, the catcher should position himself directly behind home plate and shift to the inside or outside of the strike zone in a normal fashion.

Although it generally takes a pitcher several of these sessions to solve what amounts to a serious problem, he may be successful after only one session. The key is for the pitcher to concentrate on the catcher or the catcher's mitt as his target. In reality, if the pitcher can develop confidence in hitting the catcher's mitt, it will not matter where the catcher positions himself.

DRILL #46: TARGET WITH CATCHER

Objective: To improve the pitcher's level of control.

Description: This drill is best done in a bullpen setting. The goal for the pitcher is to hit the catcher's mitt. The catcher should center his body behind his mitt and offer as big a target as possible. He should also respond on each pitch, showing enthusiasm when the pitcher hits his spot and disappointment when he does not. Regardless, the catcher's reaction is one example of his value to the pitcher as a teaching aid. Another reason the catcher is helpful to the pitcher during throwing drills is that, unlike a stationary target, he can change the pitcher's target from pitch to pitch.

Although this drill can be set up several ways, it is the ability of the pitcher that will be the greatest determining factor in the success of the exercise. The pitcher's primary objective might be to just throw strikes below the waist, or maybe the pitcher wants to practice hitting either a high or a low target. Regardless, an important factor in this drill is for the pitcher to be able to split the strike zone into halves, high and low. As the pitcher's skill level improves, he then breaks the strike zone into even smaller parts, with each part becoming a target. In the end, this target drill can be as simple or as tough as the parties involved wish to make it.

An imaginary batting order can also be added to upgrade the concentration level of the pitcher and to raise the drill's degree of difficulty. This "lineup" can provide the pitcher and the catcher with an opportunity to deal with the purported strengths and weaknesses of each hitter.

DRILL #47: DOUBLE CATCHER

Objective: To help the pitcher who has difficulty throwing to either the outside or the inside of the plate; to improve the pitcher's arm extension and his right-to-left action.

Description: Occasionally a pitcher will sell himself on the idea that he cannot throw to a particular part of the strike zone without making drastic adjustments. This drill is designed to show him that he can throw pitches inside or outside by making mostly mental adjustments and very few physical adjustments. After using this drill, the pitcher should gain confidence in his ability to throw to either side of the plate. Two catchers are needed for this drill. Normally the bullpen area has at least two mounds, which are eight to 10 feet apart. If two mounds are not available, this drill should be set up either on flat ground or at the mound on the playing field. If there are at least two mounds in the bullpen, one pitcher and one catcher should line up normally, while an extra catcher should position himself behind the other home plate, as though he were warming up another pitcher. The catchers should be eight to 10 feet apart. Throughout this drill the pitcher should alternate his throwing direction, making one throw to the catcher who is lined up in a normal bullpen position and one throw to the other catcher.

If the pitcher is right-handed and having difficulty throwing inside, he should position himself so that the extra catcher is behind the plate and to the pitcher's left side. Regardless of the catcher he selects, the pitcher should always place his stride foot in the same spot. For him to hit the target to his far left, the pitcher must make a mental adjustment. After all, he will not be required to change his stride. Only his release point will change slightly. In order to throw to the extra catcher, though, the pitcher must maintain a good right-to-left action. If warranted, the extra catcher may be positioned behind the plate, to the right of the pitcher. In this case, with only two mounds in use, the regular catcher would then become the extra catcher, and the pitcher would be required to move the rubber to his left. For the pitcher to throw to a catcher who is positioned eight to 10 feet to the left or right of the normal target, he must exhibit great arm extension. To guarantee success in this drill, the fingers of the pitcher's throwing hand must get on top of the ball.

DRILL #48: CONTROL AND CHART

Objective: To help the pitcher focus on his control and, at the same time, provide a goal for his next outing.

Description: Too often, pitchers throw in the bullpen without having specific goals. While they might like to improve on their control, speed, stuff, and all the other essential aspects of pitching, they don't have defined goals. To improve his level of control, the pitcher must commit to and concentrate on his particular goal. Toward this end, by assigning himself a number of pitches and charting the number he throws for strikes, the pitcher can start his journey to improvement. If, for instance, he throws 35 pitches—including 10 strikes—he now knows the number that would indicate improvement. By charting every bullpen pitch, he can easily see how well he is progressing toward achieving a specific goal. As his control improves, the pitcher should make his target smaller. Subsequently, as the pitcher's ability to throw strikes improves, he may shrink his zone even more by counting only those pitches in the lower part of the strike zone. All factors considered, the more advanced the pitcher, the more he can shrink his strike zone.

When charting for control, the pitcher should include all of his pitches. He should throw a certain percentage of fastballs and a certain percentage of breaking balls. His practice pitches should correlate to his game percentages.

PITCHER'S BULLPEN CONTROL CHART

NAME _____ Date _____

Number Pitches _____ Number Strikes _____

Number Fast Balls _____ Number Sliders _____

Number Change-ups _____ Percentage _____

Number Sliders _____ Percentage _____

DRILL #49: THREE FASTBALLS, THREE BREAKING BALLS

Objective: To help the pitcher develop a variety of pitches and to learn to control those pitches while throwing to a batter.

Description: This drill is a batting-practice-type exercise with emphasis on the various pitches thrown by the pitcher. The drill involves having the pitcher throw to a catcher on the regular diamond. The setting is similar to pregame batting practice, with the pitcher throwing to a hitter. The pitcher throws three fastballs and three curveballs, but he is limited to a specific number of pitches overall. The pitcher's task is to throw each pitch for a strike. Of course, the hitter's job is to make good contact. Most pitchers do not throw enough to live hitters. As a result, some have more success in the bullpen than in the game. This challenging drill familiarizes the pitcher with the game situation and puts pressure on him—if the pitcher does not get the ball over the plate, the hitter will let him know. At the very least, this drill gives the pitcher and the coach a yardstick for the pitcher's level of progress.

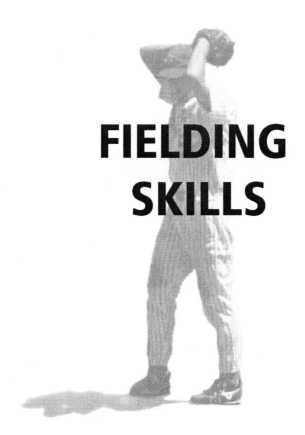

CHAPTER 6

FIELDING
SKILLS

DRILL #50: PITCHER COVERING FIRST BASE AND COMMUNICATING WITH THE FIRST BASEMAN

Objective: To help the pitcher learn to cover first base properly; to help the pitcher know his fielding area, how to call for the ball, and how to field the ball.

Description: The drill involves placing all of the pitchers in a line, starting at the pitcher's mound. All of the first basemen are also positioned in a line, starting in the normal fielding position for a first baseman. The following rules that apply to game situations should be explained to all participants in the drill:

→ The first baseman is the captain on any play between himself and the pitcher.

→ Both the first baseman and the pitcher should want to field every ball.

→ If the pitcher is to field the ball, he should call for it within three steps after his follow-through.

→ The first baseman should count to three as he takes three steps toward the ball. After the third count, if the pitcher has not yet called for the ball, the first baseman should yell, "Ball!" and field the ball.

→ If the first baseman calls for the ball, the pitcher should cover the bag.

→ Whoever fields the ball should use the term "Ball!" Whoever covers the bag should yell, "Bag!"

→ The ball should be called first. "Bag!" is the secondary call.

→ If both the pitcher and the first baseman call for the ball at the same time, the first baseman should field the ball and the pitcher should cover the bag.

→ If the pitcher covers the bag, he should run directly to the cutout of the grass nearest the base line and first base. He should then turn, run to the bag, and tag it with his right foot while awaiting or receiving the throw.

→ If the first baseman is ready to throw the ball before the pitcher gets to the bag, he may lead the pitcher with his throw. The pitcher should then catch the ball and tag the base with his right foot.

→ This drill should be run at full, or game, speed.

The coach fungoes all kinds of ground balls to and between the active pitcher and the active fielder. Each pitcher should have a ball when he gets to the front of the line. With his normal throwing motion, the pitcher then pitches to a catcher or shagger behind home plate. The coach times the pitch and fungoes ground balls as each pitcher's throw arrives at home plate.

As the drill progresses, the coach should make sure each player adheres to the rules. If mistakes are made by either the pitcher or the first baseman, the drill should be stopped and the mistake corrected. Success will take some work and a great deal of persistence and commitment.

This drill can be made easy or very difficult, depending on where and how the ball is hit. A ball hit at either player at a soft speed is easy. In this instance, communication is relatively simple. The ball is easy to field. No one is challenged on this play. Initially, the drill should start with these kinds of fungoes. As the rules are learned and applied, play can be made more difficult. For example, the placement and the speed of the batted ball can be varied. The point the coach should remember is to make the drill challenging enough to match the ability level of the respective players.

During the drill, the starting position of the first baseman should also be varied. He should initially start at his regular position, then move to his position when holding a runner at first, and finally, assume his position when faced with a bases-loaded situation.

DRILL #51: PITCHER COVERING FIRST BASE ON A BALL HIT BETWEEN THE FIRST BASEMAN AND THE SECOND BASEMAN

Objective: To improve communication and fielding techniques between the pitcher, the first baseman, and the second baseman.

Description: All the pitchers form a line, starting at the mound. The back of the line is toward left field. Each pitcher should have a ball. All the first basemen and all the second basemen form lines at their respective positions. This drill begins with the coach at home plate fungoing balls between second base and first base. The ball should be called for, fielded, and thrown to first base. First base should be covered by one of three position players. It is usually covered by the pitcher or the first baseman, but on bunt plays could be covered by the second baseman.

Before the coach (at home plate) hits any ground balls, the following rules of the drill should be explained to all drill participants:

→ The first baseman has fielding priority over the pitcher.

→ The first baseman and the second baseman should both go to the ball, unless the ball is hit directly to one of them.

→ The player who has the best angle and who is in the best throwing position should call for and field the ball.

→ Whoever fields the ball is responsible for making a call. The call (term) to use is "Ball!"

→ Someone, either the first baseman or the pitcher, normally covers the bag at first. One of the three players should call to indicate who will cover that base. The word "bag" should be shouted after the word "ball." It should be kept in mind, however, that the decision as to who will field the ball should be the primary concern. The call for who will cover the base is a secondary command. Although the primary call concerning the ball is important, the secondary call for covering the bag should not be overlooked.

→ The pitcher, if covering first base, should sprint directly to the grass cutout nearest the bag and the base line. He should run parallel to the base line on the way to the base. He should then tag the base with his right foot.

→ If the throw is ready before the pitcher reaches the base, the fielder should lead the pitcher with the throw. In this instance, the pitcher should catch the ball and then step on the bag with his right foot.

→ If the pitcher arrives at the bag and the ball is late, he should place his right foot on the bag and wait for the ball.

→ After completing the play at first, the player should disengage from the bag, move to the inside of the diamond, and prepare himself for the next play, should there be one.

This drill involves a special routine: Each pitcher makes a throw to the plate. As the ball arrives, the coach fungoes a ball between the first baseman and the second baseman. One of these two players makes a call for the ball, fields it, and throws to the pitcher covering the bag at first. The catcher or shagger flips the ball—thrown by the pitcher—to the coach, and the pitcher keeps the ball he caught while covering first base. That pitcher then goes to the end of the line, and the drill continues.

The coach should vary the direction and speed of the ground balls he hits. He should challenge the three position players to the degree that is appropriate for their ability level.

DRILL #52: PITCHER COVERING FIRST BASE TO COMPLETE DOUBLE PLAY

Objective: To help the pitcher turn the double play when the first baseman is drawn away from the bag to field a ground ball.

Description: The pitchers, first basemen, and shortstops are active participants in this drill. Each group forms a line at its respective position. The back of the line of pitchers extends toward third base. Before the drill begins, the following rules should be explained to all participants:

→ On any ball hit to the right side of the infield, the pitcher should move to first base in case he needs to cover the bag.

→ The first baseman is responsible for making the secondary call to cover the bag. If he can field, throw the ball, and get back in time for the relay throw from the shortstop, he may do so. In such a case, he calls for the ball, throws to the shortstop, and yells, "Bag!" The pitchers, who are in the area, say, "Take it!" The first baseman then makes the catch.

→ On potential double plays, the pitcher should run in a straight line to first base and set up like a first baseman. If he is to cover the bag, he so indicates by yelling, "Bag!"

→ After the play is completed at first base, the player covering that base should come off the bag and move to the inside part of the diamond and get ready for another play, should there be one.

→ If the first baseman is playing deep, he should throw the ball to the shortstop and outside of the baserunner.

→ If the first baseman is playing in a shallow position, his throw should be to the shortstop, but to the inside of the baserunner.

→ The drill should be run at full speed.

This drill begins with each pitcher taking his turn throwing a pitch to a shagger or the catcher at home plate. The coach should time each pitcher's throw. When the throw gets to the plate, the coach hits a ground ball to the first baseman. After the ball is hit, the pitcher breaks to cover first base. The first baseman then throws the ball to the shortstop. Next, the shortstop relays his throw back to first base to the pitcher who is covering the bag. If the first baseman can cover the bag after making the throw, he may do so. After the ball arrives at first base to complete the double play attempt, the ball at first is flipped to the pitcher, who trots to the end of the pitching line. The ball thrown to the shagger or catcher is flipped to the coach. The drill continues in this fashion.

DRILL #53: BUNTED BALL BETWEEN THE
THIRD BASEMAN AND THE PITCHER

Objective: To help the pitcher and the other infielders improve communication between themselves while defending against the bunt; to improve the pitcher's and other infielder's judgment, timing, agility, and throwing accuracy in a bunt situation.

Description: Although this particular drill is designed to defend the bunt with runners on first and second bases, it will also help in the defense of bunting in general. All the pitchers form a line that starts at the pitching rubber and extends toward second base. Each pitcher should have a baseball. Meanwhile, all between themselves, the third basemen form a line at third base, while a first baseman or a shagger covers first base and a catcher or a shagger covers home plate. Before the drill begins, the following defensive rules for this play must be established:

→ The third baseman takes four steps from third base toward second base and two steps inside the foul line. On this particular bunt only, he holds that position until the ball is bunted. Once it is bunted, he takes three steps toward the bunted ball.

→ The third baseman has priority on the bunt. He may allow the pitcher three steps, or three counts, to call the ball. If the pitcher does not call, the third baseman should field the bunt.

→ The pitcher should break directly toward the third-base line at a spot midway between third base and home plate. He should try to field everything from the middle of the mound to the midway spot and in. He should not, however, field or attempt to field bunts in other areas.

→ Either the third baseman or the pitcher should make a call for the ball. If the pitcher yells "Ball!", then he should be allowed to field the ball without interference.

→ The pitcher should make his call for the ball within three steps after his follow-through.

→ Ideally, the pitcher should field the ball on his glove side, then pivot and throw to third.

→ The drill should be run at game speed.

Once the rules have been established, the drill may begin. The pitcher starts the drill by throwing to the catcher or shagger at home plate. When the pitch reaches the plate, the coach fungoes a bunt toward third base. In this defensive setup, the pitcher should field the ball in order to get the force out at third. After all, he is responsible for covering the area from the mound to the third-base line and in. Although the first baseman is not included in this drill, it is his responsibility to cover the area between the first-base line and the mound.

DRILL #54: BACK-UP THROWS FROM CENTER FIELD TO THIRD BASE

Objective: To enhance on the pitcher's pickoff move to second base, as well as his ability to back up third base on a throw from the outfield.

Description: All of the outfielders should line up in center field. All of the pitchers, meanwhile, should form a line on the mound, with the back of the line extending toward right field. Each pitcher should have a ball. In addition, all of the shortstops and third basemen should form a line at their respective positions.

The drill should be conducted in the following manner: The first pitcher in line takes a stretch position. He then uses one of his pickoff moves to throw to the shortstop, who is covering second base. The pitcher should try to make an accurate throw. The shortstop should move to the bag while working on the proper timing for the pickoff. Even though the shortstop has positioned himself to field the throw, he should nonetheless allow the throw to go on into the outfield. The first outfielder, who should be backing up the pickoff throw, should then field the ball and throw it to third base. The pitcher's assignment is to move quickly and deeply behind third base. He should get as much depth as possible and align himself with the third baseman and the throw. The pitcher becomes the last line of defense on this play. His job is to either catch the ball or keep it from going out of bounds to prevent any base runners from advancing.

This procedure should be repeated for each pickoff attempt. The drill is designed not only to benefit the pitchers, but also the other position players. The pitchers should work carefully both on pickoff plays and on the fundamentals of covering bases. Proper positioning and hustle are the keys to learning the latter. Covering the bases requires hustle. To be a fully beneficial drill, a full-speed effort is necessary.

DRILL #55: PITCHER COVERING HOME PLATE

Objective: To improve the ability of the pitcher and catcher to effectively communicate on wild pitches and passed balls so that home plate is properly covered.

Description: All the pitchers should form a line beginning at the pitching rubber. Each pitcher should have a ball. The catchers, in full gear, should form a line near, but well to the side of, home plate. The drill begins with the pitcher throwing a low pitch in front of the catcher, which the catcher tries to block. The key in this instance is for the pitcher to communicate with the catcher and cover home plate if necessary. The pitcher should use hand signals and loud vocal messages to help the catcher in an instance like this. If the ball is in front of, or slightly behind, the catcher, the pitcher should point with his pitching hand to the ground in front of the catcher and yell, "In front! In front!" This hand and verbal signal means that the catcher should not turn around. Instead, he should take steps backward and concentrate on the area in front of his body.

For the ball that requires the catcher to turn, the pitcher should point upward with his pitching hand and yell, "Back!, Back!" If the ball is to the catcher's left, the pitcher should point in the direction of the ball and yell "Third base! Third base!" If the ball is to the catcher's right, the pitcher should point to the catcher's right with his glove hand. In addition, he yells, "First base! First base!" As the pitcher signals and gives verbal directions, he should move in quickly and cover home plate. When he arrives at home plate, the pitcher should align himself with the throw from the catcher, receive the throw, and make the tag by dropping to his right knee. He should make a sweep-type tag. After the tag, he should stand up and move away from the area, looking for another play. This drill should be repeated until the pitcher and the catcher have mastered the fundamentals involved.

DRILL #56: BACK-UP

Objective: To teach the pitcher how to back up a base properly; to enhance the pitcher's level of stamina.

Description: During the alignment drills for outfielders and infielders, the pitchers can be incorporated into the drill by backing up bases. This practice not only gives the pitcher a good physical workout, but also helps teach him the proper way to cover the base. In this drill, the pitcher should be required to cover the proper base, get to the coverage area quickly, and make sure his alignment is correct. During the drill, the many aspects of covering a base can be taught (e.g., the pitcher's route, spacing, and alignments). The pitcher must learn to recognize which base to cover in each particular situation. Covering the base quickly is equally important. The urgency of the pitcher being able to get to his destination quickly is an essential aspect of sound defensive team play.

DRILL #57: AROUND THE INFIELD WITH PITCHERS

Objective: To improve the defensive skills and techniques of the pitcher.

Description: This drill is a combination of many drills that have already been described. The drill takes the pitcher around the infield to each position, starting at first base, and works on defensive plays concerning the pitcher and that particular infielder. The pitcher should spend about six minutes at each position. This drill involves the following steps:

→ Pitcher and first baseman—fielding the ball and covering first base.

→ Pitcher, first baseman, and second baseman—working on ground balls between the second baseman and the first baseman, with the pitcher or the first baseman covering first base.

→ Pitcher, first baseman, and shortstop—fielding double-play grounders starting with the first baseman, who throws to the shortstop, who relays back to first base with the pitcher covering.

→ Pitcher and third baseman—working on bunt defense with runners at first and second.

→ Pitcher, shortstop, center fielder, and third baseman—working on the center fielder backing up a pickoff throw from the pitcher and throwing to third, where the pitcher backs up.

→ Pitcher and catcher—working on the catcher blocking low pitches, on communication between the pitcher and the catcher, and on the pitcher covering home plate.

This drill, if done properly, will help the pitching staff in particular, but it will also greatly improve the overall team defense. This drill was designed in the 1940s by Pete Beiden, a legendary baseball coach from Fresno State University. It was sound then, and it is sound today. Beiden recommended using this drill once a week, and spending about 45 minutes on it.

DRILL #58: THREE-IN-ONE

Objective: To help the pitcher improve his fundamentals in four different defensive plays: covering first base, fielding a ground ball to start the double play, backing up third base, and pitching out to the catcher; to help the catcher with his pitchout footwork and his throw to second base.

Description: This drill is a defensive exercise that involves every player on the team. All of the players should be in their respective positions, with the exception of the outfielders, who should form one line in center field. Two fungo hitters should be positioned at home plate, one to the right of the catcher and the other to the left of the catcher. Before starting the drill, the coach should explain each segment to the fielders and emphasize that for safety reasons, all return throws must go to their proper destinations without placing anyone in harm's way.

The drill starts with the first pitcher in line throwing to the catcher. As the ball approaches the plate, the fungo hitter to the right of the catcher hits a ground ball between first and second base. The pitcher covers first base. He keeps the ball and returns to the end of the pitching line. The next pitcher then throws to the catcher as soon as the previous pitcher has cleared the area. As his throw approaches the plate, the other fungo hitter hits a ground ball to that pitcher. The pitcher fields the ball, turns, and attempts to make an accurate throw to second base. The shortstop, who is covering the bag, lets the ball go into the outfield. The pitcher waits until the ball hits the outfield grass and then sprints to back up third base. The center fielder backs up the play and throws to third base. After covering the bag at second and letting the ball go into the outfield, the shortstop moves into position and becomes the cutoff man. The pitcher's timing on this play should be the same as in a game.

The next pitcher in line practices his pitchout delivery and throws to the catcher as soon as the previous pitcher has cleared the area. On this pitch, the catcher works on his footwork for a pitchout and throws to second base. A second baseman or a shortstop catches the throw.

This drill takes the pitcher through four very important defensive plays. Each pitcher should have already been schooled on each play before engaging in the combination of drills.

DRILL #59: COMEBACKERS TO THE PITCHER

Objective: To help the pitcher field different kinds of ground balls and make the various throws that are necessary for different types of plays.

Description: The pitchers should form a line on the mound. The pitcher at the head of the line takes his position on the pitching rubber. The line should flow in the direction of third base, and only the active pitcher in the drill should be on the mound.

The drill can be done in several different ways. One approach is to have the pitcher work on fielding the ground ball and simulating the throw to first base. In this instance, careful attention should be paid to fielding and footwork in the simulated throwing portion. This scenario is a particularly good teaching method for younger players or for introducing the fielding fundamentals. On the other hand, both the beginning pitcher and the experienced pitcher can profit from this drill.

This drill is particularly helpful to the pitcher who has control problems when the first baseman is not ready to receive his throw. In this specific instance, the pitcher should take a step and reset his hands for throwing. He may need to reset more than once on some throws. In those cases, he simply takes another step and resets until the first baseman is ready to receive his throw.

Some pitchers have difficulties making short-distance throws; their tendency is to aim, let up on the throw, or do both. Because of its repetitiveness, this drill can have a positive impact on helping to correct this type of throwing flaw.

Adding a first baseman and including live throwing can provide another dimension to the drill and give the pitcher a chance to practice and improve the different kinds of throws required. The coach who is hitting fungoes can control the degree of difficulty by the way he hits the ball. He can, for example, switch from routine, one-hop ground balls hit straight to the pitcher to firmly hit balls that stretch the fielding range of the pitcher.

DRILL #60: PITCHER'S POP FLY

Objective: To improve the ability of the pitcher to effectively communicate with his infielders on pop-ups.

Description: The drill is set up with the catchers in a line behind home plate and the first basemen in a line at first base. The pitchers, meanwhile, form a line on the mound. The coach is stationed at home plate with a fungo bat, where he hits pop flies between the first baseman and the catcher.

It is the responsibility of the players at these two positions (catcher and first baseman) to communicate with each other on the pop-up, while the pitcher acts as a helper on the call. If, for instance, the first baseman has priority and has called for the ball, the pitcher should yell, "First base! First base!" and move in front of the catcher. This move gives the catcher a clear picture of who should catch the pop fly. For the pitcher to be included in the communication process, of course, it is necessary for him to know the pop-fly priority system. The important point that should be emphasized is that the pitcher can be of great assistance to his teammates on defense if he communicates properly on pop flies.

DRILL #61: POP FLY WITH RUNNERS AT FIRST AND THIRD

Objective: To improve the ability of the pitcher to react to a pop-up deep behind home plate or in foul territory near first or third.

Description: On this play, if the runners both tag, the infielders have a tough decision to make. If the runner at first base tags and starts to second base thereby drawing the throw to second, the runner tagging at third will score. If the runner at third tags, drawing a throw to home plate, the runner tagging at first can advance to second base. To work on this play, the coach sets up the defense and places runners at first and third. He then hits pop flies and instructs the runners to tag and draw a throw. The basic guidelines for the pitcher on this play are as follows: if the ball is hit deep behind home plate, the pitcher sprints in and covers the plate. The catcher fields the pop fly and quickly turns and throws to the pitcher, who is covering the plate. This throw will freeze the runner at third. At this point, the pitcher can turn and throw to second, hopefully in time to get the runner attempting to advance from first base after having tagged up.

If the pop fly is hit in foul territory and deep in the first-base area, the pitcher sprints over and covers first base, where he receives the throw from the first baseman after the pop fly is fielded. If this play does not freeze the runner at first, the pitcher may throw to second, or he may throw home if the runner at third base tags and tries to advance. If the pop fly is hit deep in foul territory near third base, the pitcher should sprint to third base and cover the bag. He will receive the throw from the third baseman after the pop fly is caught. He then either throws to home plate or to second base.

DRILL #62: PITCHERS' BASES LOADED

Objective: To practice and successfully develop the skills necessary for a pitcher to quickly and accurately make the play to home with the bases loaded and to make the double play.

Description: In this drill, the pitcher is on the mound, while the catcher is in full gear behind the plate. The first baseman should play shallow. When the ball is hit back to the pitcher, he throws the ball to the catcher. The catcher tags home plate and then throws to the first baseman for the second part of the double play. In this drill, the pitcher is required to field many different kinds of ground balls and to adjust his throwing accordingly.

When the pitcher becomes adept at making a good throw on a routine ground ball, other types of ground balls should be added to the drill. For example, the one-hop, come-back-type of ground ball may be especially difficult for the pitcher. Therefore, the coach should increase the degree of difficulty of the grounders he hits as the pitcher's skill level warrants. As a consequence, he will present the pitcher with the need to throw from a variety of positions. A high-hop ground ball that may result in only a force play is one such throw. This situation requires a good fielding position as well as a quick, short throw. Some back-hand plays also present a challenge for some pitchers. On this type of play, the pitcher must field the ball, get into a balanced position, try to get into a good throwing angle, and throw accurately to the plate. The point to keep in mind is that the coach should make sure the pitcher has a well-rounded diet of ground balls during this drill.

To make the drill even more challenging, the coach can conduct the drill live—with base runners and defensive players. In this setting, the coach should not always hit the ball back to the pitcher; instead, he should hit it to one of the other infielders. This approach will make the drill more game-like.

CHAPTER 7

PICKOFF MOVES

DRILL #63: HEEL-UP PICKOFF

Objective: To help the pitcher develop a sound heel-up pickoff move.

Description: The pitchers should form no more than two lines, with each line small enough so that each pitcher is in the coach's line of sight. Each pitcher starts in a stretch position, with his front shoulder closed and pointing at the coach or the target.

The pitcher starts the drill by clearing his push-off foot from the pitching rubber, a move that will require the lifting of his heel. In this drill, the pitcher raises this heel slightly as he opens and strides to throw to first base—a smooth and quick move. Once he is able to perform this move satisfactorily, he should include the other important elements of throwing that he has been practicing, including correctly separating his hands and getting the ball into throwing position.

As he lifts his heel and begins to turn his foot, the pitcher's hands should separate. On a normal move to the plate, the pitcher's hands move up slightly and then fall to separation at or near his belt. On the pickoff move, however, his pitching hand should be released from his glove by lifting the ball above the glove. Thus, as the pitcher lifts his push-off heel and as he begins to spin to an open stance, he lifts the ball above his glove. Because balance throughout the pickoff move is very important, the pitcher should carefully coordinate the pickoff maneuver. He really should first work on this action in a dry-run setting until his movement becomes balanced, well timed, and coordinated.

The next part of this drill is to add live throwing. To do this, the pitchers are paired up and separated approximately 60 feet apart. The pitcher making the throw aligns himself as though he were on the mound and acts as though the drill includes the first baseman. Once set, the pitcher practices his pickoff move. If live throwing presents problems, the pitcher can go back to the dry-run setting. As a matter of fact, he should move back and forth from dry-run to live throwing until he is successfully able to properly perform a heel-up pickoff move with live throwing.

All of this practice is meant to help the pitcher perfect a pickoff for game situations. The next step in the drill is to take the drill to the mound and include the first baseman. It is at this point that the pitcher's pickoff move can truly be evaluated. Some pitchers will need to return to a dry run or to practice throws. Others will be ready to work a few minutes each day with the first baseman to perfect the timing of the pickoff move. The final test is the game. Without question, diligent work on the heel-up pickoff move will pay off in game situations.

When the heel-up pickoff is attempted at second base, the pitcher should use the same procedure, except that the push-off foot must make a wider turn to throw to second. The pitcher should make sure his weight shift and pivot are correct before live throwing is included.

DRILL #64: JUMP-TURN PICKOFF

Objective: To improve the ability of the pitcher to execute a jump-turn pickoff.

Description: In this drill, the pitchers form one or two lines. Each pitcher must be in the coach's line of sight. The pitchers assume a stride position and then start the drill by simulating the pickoff move. Each pitcher activates his pickoff move by jumping in the air with both feet. He rotates his body toward first base, landing on his push-off foot with his throwing hand ready, and then strides and throws to the base. Before completing the entire move, the pitcher should first practice the jump move. To make the jump move, the pitcher's knees should not be bent dramatically. The jump requires only a slight, unnoticeable drop. In fact, if the bending of the knees is too noticeable, a balk may result. Initially, the correct move by the pitcher is to begin with a slight bend at the knee and then continue by jumping and opening up toward first base. The pitcher's body should be rotated about a quarter of a turn.

When the pitcher can satisfactorily operate the jump move, he should then include the proper hand movement. The pitcher's hand movement should begin as the pitcher jumps. During his jump, he separates his hands by lifting the ball above his glove. Next, he takes the ball from his glove by lifting and moving it directly to a ready position. Once his push-off foot hits the ground after the jump, he begins his throw. The pitcher should practice the jump turn until he has mastered it, and then practice it with live throwing.

For live throwing, the pitchers should be paired up. One partner will act as a first baseman, while the other will act as the pitcher. The pitcher practicing the jump move should position himself so that his partner is at the angle of a first baseman. He should then practice live throwing. If throwing creates too much of a problem, the pitcher should eliminate it. The important thing is that the pitcher should practice the simulated pick-off move until he is able to achieve a proper degree of balance, rhythm, and timing. Once the pitcher feels confident with this part of the drill, he should then add the throw.

For the final part of the drill, the first baseman is involved. Initially from the pitching rubber, the pitcher practices the jump turns with the first baseman. At each level of the drill, the coach should evaluate the pitcher. Although practicing with the first baseman is ideal, some pitchers may find this part of the drill too challenging. Therefore, they should continue to work with the beginning phases of the drill. By improving his basic maneuvers, the pitcher will be better equipped to achieve at a more challenging pace. Above all, the pitcher should develop a solid base and use that base to move through the drill and enhance his ability to achieve his primary objective—to take a good jump-turn pickoff move into the game.

The jump turn can be used in the same manner at second base. The pitcher, however, needs to work with both the shortstop and the second baseman on that particular pickoff. To accomplish a successful jump turn to second base, a greater rotation, or turn, is necessary. The pitcher uses the same techniques to jump, but instead of a quarter turn to get in line with first base, he must make a half turn in order to align his body to throw to second base. The pitcher should keep in mind that he still starts his turn toward first base. By all means, the pitcher should first be able to execute the proper move to first base before taking on the move to second base. He should also understand, however, that the pickoff move to first base will make his pickoffs at other bases easier.

DRILL #65: QUICK TO THE PLATE

Objective: To help the pitcher polish and improve his movements from the stretch position; to help the pitcher speed up his delivery to the plate.

Description: The pitchers should form no more than two lines, with each pitcher in the coach's line of sight. Each pitcher begins the drill by starting in the stretch position and then simulating the throwing motion. The coach should review and evaluate each pitcher's stance and make sure the pitcher's feet are close together and in a closed position. As he practices the leg lift, the pitcher should pay close attention to the proper angle of his leg and the speed of his leg lift. He should then incorporate his increased speed into his rhythm. Once he notices an improvement in his leg lift, the pitcher should concentrate on the movement and quickness of his hands. One key for the pitcher is to make sure his hands are moving through the midline of his body. Another key is for the pitcher to work on moving and separating his hands as efficiently as possible, with little, if any, wasted movement. Because quicker hands are also softer hands, the pitcher should practice his hand movement diligently.

Movements from the stretch should be quick, fluid, and functional. It takes work to coordinate the movements in the stretch position. As the drill progresses, pair up the pitchers and have them work on the movements of the delivery to the plate by throwing to each other. It is interesting to note that the optimum time for the ball to reach the bat or the catcher's mitt—clocked from the pitcher's first move from the stretch—is 1.3 seconds.

DRILL #66: STEP-OFF AND PICKOFF

Objective: To have the pitcher practice stepping off the rubber and then executing a pickoff to disrupt the baserunner's timing; to teach the pitcher how to disengage from the mound, pause, and then execute an effective pickoff move to first base.

Description: In this drill, the pitchers form one or two lines. Each pitcher must be in the line of sight of the pitching coach. Each pitcher should practice the drill from his stretch position. The first portion of the drill should be practiced and understood before the pitcher advances to other situations. The drill begins by having the entire pitching group move into the stretch position, raise their hands, and come to a set position. Next, the pitchers quickly lift their push-off foot and step off the rubber. This part of the drill is repeated until each pitcher can easily and smoothly accomplish the move.

In the next part of the drill, each pitcher steps back off the rubber, pauses, and throws to first base for an attempted pickoff. He should repeat this procedure a few times and, at the same time, vary the length of the pause. Each pitcher should develop three or four different patterns, for example, step back and throw over immediately; step back, cadence count 1,001 before throwing to first; step back, count 1,001, 1,002, and then pickoff at first; or step back, cadence count 1,001, 1,002, 1,003, and pickoff. The important point emphasized in this situation is that the pitcher should change his timing pattern to disrupt the timing pattern of the baserunner.

The pitcher should use either the heel-up and turn or the jump turn to make the throw to first base. He should also practice the different cadence counts and the pickoff move until the move can be incorporated into his arsenal for game use.

DRILL #67: BARR PICKOFF (RIGHT-HANDED PITCHERS ONLY)

Objective: To develop and perfect the Barr pickoff (a special pickoff move).

Description: The pitchers form one or two lines. Each pitcher should be within line of sight of the instructor. Each pitcher should work from the stretch position. The pitcher starts the drill by stepping back and off the pitching rubber, but the direction his push-off foot takes will be different from the regular step-off-and-throw-to-first pickoff. In the Barr pickoff move, the pitcher steps back to disengage from the rubber, but he adds a new dimension to the average pickoff move by stepping off in the direction of third base. With his push-off foot free of the rubber and planted toward third, the pitcher has almost positioned himself to throw to first base, although he is still in a closed position. To open and throw to first, he must turn, spin on his stride-foot heel, and throw. This maneuver, which is somewhat awkward at the outset, underscores the importance of position and balance. The pitcher should try to achieve both as he sets his push-off foot after disengaging from the rubber. The pitcher is establishing the length of his stride by where he places his push-off foot, and it is this foot placement that also plays a major role in his alignment toward first base. The pitcher should practice this maneuver in a dry-run setting and then practice it with live throwing to a partner. Once his Barr pickoff move is adequate in these settings, the pitcher should include the first baseman for a game-like environment.

DRILL #68: PICKOFF AND TIMING

Objective: To help the pitcher develop different methods to disrupt the baserunner's timing, including using his head as a way to slow the jump of the baserunner and learning to use time as a weapon.

Description: The drill can be executed in three settings. The first setting calls for simulating the moves. The second setting requires live throwing to each other. The third setting involves live throwing from the mound to a first baseman. The drill involves placing the pitchers in one or two lines, making sure the instructor can see each pitcher. Each pitcher practices the drill from the stretch position. Each pitcher should go into the stretch as though he is holding a runner at first, and then come to a set position, look over to first, turn his head back to the target, and simulate a throw to home plate. The pitcher should repeat this procedure for a few throws.

Next the pitcher should come to a set position, look to first, look to home, look to first, look to home, and simulate a throw to home plate. He should then repeat this procedure for a few throws.

Finally, have the pitchers add a third look to first and a third look to home before throwing to the plate. The pitcher may disrupt the timing of the baserunner by looking either once, twice, or three times and then back to the plate before throwing. By varying the number of looks to first base, the pitcher can interfere with the runner's timing.

One other possible variation for the drill is to have the pitcher look to first, look to home, and then pick off at first base. He should practice this move a few times, and then add two looks and three looks to the drill.

By looking and counting, the pitcher can further disrupt the baserunner. In one such timing pattern, the pitcher should practice looking quickly to first, looking back to home plate, and holding the count before throwing. He should also practice looking and counting at different speeds. Most importantly, the pitcher should vary his timing and looks. The pitcher should keep practicing in a simulated setting until he develops a relatively high degree of comfort. In other words, the pitcher should be able to perform a pickoff throw without negatively affecting his pitching motion.

CHAPTER 8

WARMING UP
AND CONDITIONG

DRILL #69: CONDITIONING AND GROUND BALLS

Objective: To provide the pitcher with sufficient running to improve or sustain his level of conditioning; to provide the pitcher with the opportunity to practice fielding ground balls.

Description: The pitchers form a line at the shortstop position. The line should trail toward left-center field. Each pitcher should wear his glove. The coach is stationed at home plate with two shaggers, a fungo bat, and several baseballs. One player will stand well to the side of the coach and act as a shagger. The other player will act as a feeder for the coach. The first pitcher in line runs toward the third-base line. The coach should lead the pitcher by hitting a ground ball that challenges the pitcher. Of course, the primary goal for the pitcher is to field the ball cleanly. After fielding the ball, the pitcher rolls the ball to the shagger, moves to the third-base line and forms the beginning of a line on that side of the diamond. The next pitcher in line starts running toward the third-base line as soon as the pitcher in front of him has made contact with the ground ball. He then duplicates the effort of his predecessor. Each of the other pitchers follows suit until the line of pitchers on the third-base line is complete. When the last pitcher in the third-base line fields a ground ball, the same procedure is repeated, with the pitchers running toward second base.

This drill is designed to afford the pitcher an equal opportunity to field balls to his left and to his right. Since a lot of bending and stretching are involved in running and fielding, this drill will help get, or keep, the pitcher in shape, and at the same time enhance his fielding skills.

DRILL #70: GROUND BALL RELAY

Objective: To improve the pitcher's overall level of conditioning, agility, and coordination; to enhance the pitcher's sense of competitiveness; to improve the pitcher's fielding and throwing skills.

Description: The pitchers should be divided into at least two groups, with each group forming a team that will compete against the other team. The teams should have an equal number of pitchers. Each team should divide into pairs. The competitors will race to and from a point that has been marked off at a distance of 40-50 yards. The pairs will run in relay fashion. When a pair on each team finishes its part of the race, the next pair begins.

The teams should be at least 20 feet apart. Each pair should maintain a spacing of at least 10 feet between the two of them throughout their run. Each pair should sprint the prescribed distance and return to the starting point while rolling ground balls to each other. Each team should run the course at least four times. As the players run the course, the rolling of ground balls, catching, and throwing should be continuous. As soon as the ball is caught, each pitcher must, while running, begin and complete a tossed ground ball. This ball-exchange sprint is designed to add an extra challenge to the event and to offer a chance for each pitcher to improve his fielding and throwing skills.

DRILL #71: CATCH AND THROW RELAY

Objective: To enhance the pitcher's basic level of stamina; to provide the pitcher with an opportunity to practice his catching and throwing techniques.

Description: This drill is set up and operated in the same manner as the previous drill (#70—Ground Ball Relay). The only difference between the two drills is how the ball is exchanged. In this drill, the ball should be kept in the air. Each pair of pitchers plays catch while sprinting the prescribed course.

DRILL #72: LEAD

Objective: To enhance the pitcher's overall level of stamina; to improve the pitcher's fielding skills; to sharpen the ability of the pitcher to go "all out."

Description: All the pitchers should form a line next to the coach at a designated spot near one of the foul lines. From this spot, enough room should exist to run a relatively long distance and field a thrown ball or a ball hit off a fungo bat. A good example is to start at the foul line between third base and the left-field fence. From this spot, each of the pitchers should run about 40 yards, cut to his left, and look back toward the coach. The coach then hits a fly ball that leads the pitcher. Ideally, the ball should be hit so that the pitcher is required to run relatively hard to reach it. The pitcher should return to the end of the line after catching or retrieving the fly ball. The next pitcher in line should start the same pattern, once the pitcher going for the fly ball cuts to his left. As the last pitcher in the line cuts to his left, the pitcher who originally began the drill starts a new pattern. He runs the first part of the route in the same direction, but then cuts to his right and is led by the fly ball. Subsequently, all the pitchers should complete the same route. The drill continues by alternating the routes after the line of pitchers finishes the previous route toward center field. Each pitcher should catch a fly ball and then return to the end of the line with the ball. Before the pitcher begins his pattern, he tosses his ball to the coach.

The pitchers should be required to run hard for each fly ball and make a concerted effort to catch the ball in the air. Ideally, the fungoes should be hit in a way that challenges the pitcher. While the ball should be hit within the fielding range of the pitcher, it should require a full effort for him to reach the ball.

DRILL #73: PICKUP AND RECOVERY

Objective: To encourage teamwork and competitive spirit by combining sprints with endurance.

Description: The pitchers should form groups with an equal number of pitchers in each. Two to four pitchers should be assigned to each group. Each group is, in effect, a team that competes against the other teams.

Starting at the foul line, a course is marked off by placing six gloves 10 yards apart for each team. Each team forms a line at the starting mark in front of each line of gloves. Six baseballs are also placed at the starting mark.

The drill begins on the verbal command of the coach. Upon the coach's signal, the first pitcher in each line picks up a baseball, sprints 10 yards, and places the ball in the first glove. He then turns around and sprints back. He then picks up another baseball, sprints 20 yards, and places the ball in the second glove. He sprints back and continues this process until a ball is placed in each glove. When he returns to the starting point after placing a ball in the last glove, the next pitcher in line runs to each of the gloves and brings each ball back to the starting point, picking up the balls in the same sequence they were placed in the gloves. Every other pitcher on each team puts the balls in the glove, originally every other pitcher on each team brings the balls back from the gloves. The first team to complete the sequence of activities wins the event. Every time a pitcher completes this drill, he is running 360 yards. One time through is considered a relatively good workout; twice through, an excellent workout.

DRILL #74: LEFT AND RIGHT

Objective: To maintain or improve a pitcher's level of stamina, leg strength, and flexibility; to enhance the pitcher's ability to purposely move his feet.

Description: Two spots are marked off on the field, 20 feet apart. The warning track is ideal. The fence represents one spot, and the grass edge of the warning track represents the other spot. The pitchers should form a line, with each pitcher an arm's distance apart from his adjacent teammate. Lined up on the grass edge of the warning track, the pitchers face the coach. Using the warning track as an example, the drill is conducted as follows: The coach should stand at the left-field foul line at the grass edge of the warning track. In this position, he should be facing the playing field and should be looking down the warning track toward the center-field area. The pitchers, meanwhile, should be in line and facing the coach. At the head of the line should be a pitcher who should set a challenging pace. The other pitchers should keep pace with the leader.

On the coach's command, the drill starts. The line of pitchers should use quick shuffle steps to reach the fence. When they get to the fence, they should reach down with both hands and touch the bottom of the fence. The pitchers should then do shuffle steps back to the grass edge of the warning track. At that point, they should reach down with both hands and touch the grass. Every pitcher in line who has accomplished this task is credited with one trip. By the same token, every pitcher in line who has not touched each spot with both hands should not be credited with a trip. The goal is to travel correctly, over and back, 20 times.

DRILL #75: THE TRAIN

Objective: To build the pitcher's level of stamina; to enhance the pitcher's sprinting ability.

Description: The coach should mark a running course; the baseball playing field is ideal. The pitchers form a line. The drill is started by having the line of pitchers begin to jog around the playing field, staying in foul territory. The drill then continues by having the pitcher at the back of the line sprint to the front of the line. When that pitcher reaches the front of the line, the pitcher at the end of the line sprints to the front of the line. This procedure continues until a predetermined number of repetitions around the playing field is performed. For example, ten times around the playing field would typically be considered an excellent workout.

DRILL #76: THIRTY-SECOND FOUL LINE

Objective: To help the pitcher develop and maintain his level of stamina; to improve the pitcher's sprinting ability; to enhance the pitcher's sense of self-discipline.

Description: The coach and the pitching staff start this drill at either the left- or the right-field warning track along the foul line. For example, in this drill, the starting point could be the left-field warning track. The pitchers should be divided into groups of two or three. Each group is required to run on the warning track to the right-field foul line in 30 seconds or less. On the coach's command, the first group starts. Subsequently, at 10-second intervals, each of the other groups start on the coach's command. When the last group touches the foul line in right field, the coach then signals with his hand held in the air for the groups to start the return trip. Once again, at 10-second intervals, the other groups sprint back to the original starting position. This procedure continues until each pitcher has run six foul lines. The distance from the left-field foul line to the right-field foul line is counted as one foul line.

As a rule, pitchers who are in relatively good shape can perform this drill satisfactorily. Not surprisingly, however, many players have to push a bit to stay within the time limit. This drill is a great change-of-pace exercise that can help the pitcher develop an enhanced level of self-discipline.

DRILL #77: RABBIT

Objective: To help condition the pitcher's level of anaerobic (i.e., primarily without oxygen) energy; to enhance the pitcher's sprinting ability and baserunning skills within a competitive environment.

Description: This drill involves quick bursts of speed. The base paths are designated as the running course. Eight pitchers are stationed 45 feet apart around the bases, with one pitcher at each base and one pitcher at each of the halfway points between each base and between home plate and first and third base. On the coach's signal, the pitchers begin to sprint around the bases. Each pitcher should touch each base. He should try to catch the pitcher in front of him. If he tags the runner in front of him, the pitcher tagging the runner drops out of the drill, leaving a bigger space for the pitcher behind him to cover. As the successful pitchers in this drill eliminate themselves, a greater challenge is created for those remaining in the drill.

The coach should employ common sense when conducting the drill. If only two or three pitchers remain in the drill and the distance separating them is relatively great, the drill should be stopped. This drill should be run quickly and with maximum effort. It should not be used to punish or embarrass a pitcher.

DRILL #78: FLIPPERS

Objective: To improve the pitcher's level of wrist strength, flexibility, and speed.

Description: This drill should be done every day for just a few minutes. Both wrists should be exercised. Even though the major emphasis of the drill is on the pitcher's throwing wrist, this exercise can also help enhance the level of flexibility and quickness of his glove hand as well. The drill involves three different exercise steps. The first part of the exercise entails flipping the wrist up and down, with the arm held in front of the body at full extension. The second phase is done with the arms held down to the sides at full extension. The third part is accomplished with arms held over the head, reaching skyward at full extension.

The pitcher starts the drill with his arms fully extended in front of his body, at a chest-high level. In response to a signal from the coach, the pitcher starts moving his hand up and down in a quick, exaggerated waving motion, much like the flippers on a skin diver. He should keep the arms extended and flip his wrists in a continuous motion for 30 seconds; he then rests for 30 seconds. After performing a total of four repetitions and resting for 30 seconds after each repetition, the pitcher should then do four repetitions with his arms held down at his sides (following the same procedures as he did for the repetitions with his arms fully extended). Finally, at that point, with his hands over his head and reaching skyward, the pitcher should then perform four repetitions in the same manner as the previous sets.

It is important for the pitcher to keep his arms extended during each set. The action of the wrists should be an up-and-down movement. Initially, the wrist should be moved straight back, with the backs of the fingers reaching toward the top of the forearm. Next, the wrist should be bent forward. The palm of the hand should reach for the bottom part of the forearm. Part of the success of the drill will hinge on the quickness and correctness of movement. The fingers, hands, and wrists should do the work, not the arms. By practicing this drill, the pitcher will help his wrists become supple. All factors considered, the more supple the wrist of the pitcher's throwing hand, the better release he will have.

DRILL #79: EGG ROLLS, OR PICKUPS

Objective: To help build the pitcher's level of stamina and flexibility.

Description: The pitchers pair up and face each other at a distance of 10 feet. One pitcher (the feeder) begins the drill by rolling the ball to the other pitcher (the receiver). The receiver should shuffle from side to side and travel about five to six steps in each direction before he fields the ball with both hands and tosses it back to the feeder. No glove is needed. The feeder should be in a good balance position to catch and return the ball quickly and should roll the ball in a consistent manner. The feeder should also keep track of the number of balls he rolls to the receiver.

Once the pitcher is in good physical condition, he should do about 100 repetitions of this drill daily (i.e., fielding one ball equals one repetition). At the start of the season, 25 is a sufficient number of repetitions. As a rule, this drill also involves a lot of stretching and bending.

DRILL #80: LONG TOSS

Objective: To help the pitcher stretch and strengthen the muscles of his throwing arm and shoulders.

Description: Long throwing, if done properly, can help the pitcher throw the ball farther and faster. Before doing any kind of long throwing or any kind of hard throwing, however, the pitcher should be warmed up properly and should be in shape. Unfortunately, pitchers often try to throw too hard in a game or a practice before they are physically ready to do so.

Long throwing can be used as a stretching or maintenance activity. It can also be done as a means to improve arm strength. Long throwing entails making a few throws at a distance that requires exertion but not full effort. This type of long throwing can be done once or twice a week. A throw of 270 feet by a pitcher who is capable of throwing 300 feet would be considered a maintenance throw.

For purposes of improving speed and distance, the pitcher should expend a maximum effort. For this kind of throw, the pitcher's arm must be in good physical condition. It must also be adequately warmed up. In addition, in order to make these kinds of throws, the pitcher must display good mechanics. Finally, the pitcher should make only a few throws of this type during any given workout. For this drill, five to 10 throws are recommended.

In order to organize and evaluate the pitcher's long-throwing ability, the pitcher should initially establish his "throwing mark." To determine such a mark, he simply makes five to 10 throws for distance, but without expending a maximum effort. He should then use the best of the five to 10 throws as a marker. On each succeeding session of conducting this drill, achieving a greater distance than this mark would indicate that the pitcher has achieved improvement. As a rule, most pitchers in their first few long-throwing sessions should show progress. On each succeeding long-throw practice session, the pitcher may exert more energy as he gets accustomed to the drill. After a few sessions, the pitcher can throw with a full effort on each of the five throws. At this point, the pitcher's progress will tend to come much more slowly.

As the pitcher reaches a plateau or finds increases in distance hard to achieve, his mechanics, weight training efforts, and conditioning program will begin to play even more important roles. One or all of these factors may enable the pitcher to achieve an even greater level of improvement. All factors considered, an improvement in distance will mean an improvement in speed.

DRILL #81: WRIST STRETCHER

Objective: To enhance the pitcher's level of wrist flexibility.

Description: In order to attain noticeable and lasting results, this exercise should be repeated on a regular basis. To that end, this drill calls for the pitcher to spend a few minutes each day with a series of wrist exercises, bending and stretching so that his wrists are ready to withstand the force unleashed on them when he pitches in a game. When throwing the ball, the pitcher's wrist pulls back and then snaps forward to a bent position. When the wrist goes from a bent, or forward, position to a backward position as the elbow leads, great force is unleashed with the fingers and the wrist action. As such, performing a series of stretching exercises can minimize the stressful impact on the pitcher's wrist.

As a consequence, pitchers should follow this simple routine each day: Hold their right hand out in front of their body. Pull their right wrist backward and point the fingers of that hand upward as far as possible. Take their left hand and pull the fingers of their right hand back, stretching the wrist backward. Take the wrist back as far as possible and hold for 10 seconds, then release slowly. Next, with their arm still extended, bend the wrist forward as far as possible. The fingers should be pointing downward. Try to touch the bottom part of their forearm. Place their left hand on the back of their right hand and push their wrist forward as far as possible and hold for 10 seconds, then release slowly. Repeat this process with their left wrist. Perform four repetitions with each wrist. In the maximum stretch-and-bend positions, the pitchers should be careful. They should not push unduly hard in either of the stretch positions. They should not go to the point of pain. Rather, they should bend or pull their wrist forward or backward as far as it will go, then apply a gentle push or a pull to enhance the wrist's level of flexibility.

DRILL #82: FOUL LINE RUNNING

Objective: To help the pitcher build his level of stamina.

Description: This drill is another excellent distance-running exercise that is conducted by having the pitcher run from foul line to foul line. Eighteen foul lines equal approximately one and three-quarter miles. All factors considered, completing this run can be psychologically and physiologically challenging because of the turnarounds involved. To run this in 13 minutes is comparable to running a normal two-mile course. Running the foul-line-to-foul-line course can have particular value if it is run at a steady, continuous pace without a time limit.

The coach should keep in mind that he should employ variety in the running drills he incorporates into the team's conditioning regimen. For example, long-distance running can be enhanced by running a variety of courses. If a particular course has hills, steady inclines, or other special features, the running can become both more interesting and challenging.

DRILL #83: JUMP, STRIDE, AND CLAP

Objective: To improve the pitcher's level of stamina, coordination, and balance.

Description: The pitchers form several lines facing the coach. Four or five lines with two players in each line are ideal. Enough space between each player should exist to enable each pitcher to move freely. Each pitcher starts in a stride position. He then jumps and lands with his feet changing places, and claps his hands underneath his lead knee. The pitcher should rest briefly and then repeat this drill for several repetitions.

Depending on how many repetitions of the drill are performed and how much rest the pitchers are given between repetitions, the drill can involve balance, stretching, and conditioning efforts. All factors considered, requiring the pitcher to coordinate the movements of his legs and his arms while maintaining his balance can be helpful to the pitcher.

DRILL #84: PITCHER'S AGILITY

Objective: To improve the pitcher's level of agility, balance, and conditioning.

Description: The pitchers form lines similar to those in the previous drill ("Jump, Stride, and Clap"). The drill involves having the pitchers respond to the coach's signals. The coach points down for forward movement and up for backward movement. He points to the pitcher's left for movement in that direction, and to the pitcher's right for movement in that direction.

If the movement is forward, the pitchers take between four or five regular running steps in that direction. If the movement is in any other direction, the pitchers should take four or five crossover steps. Any change of direction should be done quickly and smoothly. As a rule, three to four minutes of this activity should provide an adequate workout. The drill should be performed on a regular basis.

DRILL #85: COMPETITIVE WIND SPRINT

Objective: To enhance the pitcher's level of foot speed and stamina; to heighten the pitcher's sense of competitive spirit.

Description: This drill consists of six to 10 wind sprints of 40 to 60 yards each. The drill involves pairing the pitchers up and positioning them at the starting mark. Both players in a pair should be as equal in running speed as possible. As each pair finishes a sprint, the winner's name is called. All pairs should then return to the starting point by jogging. The amount of rest time between each of these sprint sessions should be uniform. Each race should begin as one is finished. To add variety and a sense of competition to the drill, winners of subsequent sprint races could be paired up to determine the "fastest man of the day."

DRILL #86: BASERUNNING

Objective: To enhance the pitcher's level of stamina and foot speed; to practice the pitcher's baserunning skills.

Description: The pitchers can act as baserunners during an alignment drill like this one. When the defense is drilled on extra-base hits with no one on base, the pitchers should form a line at home plate and take turns running when each double is hit to the outfield. Such an action can provide a relatively realistic picture of timing to the outfielders. As such, the pitcher should run the bases all out (i.e., with a full effort).

When the situation involves defending against the batter hitting a double with a runner at first base, the pitchers should divide into two lines. One line should be at first base, while the other line should be positioned at home plate. In the drill, the runner at first base will try to score, and the runner at home will try to advance to third on the throw to home plate. Good baserunning by the pitchers will challenge the outfielders and infielders to throw accurately and quickly. In a sense, the pitcher is helping his own cause. He is getting in shape and sharpening his baserunning skills while simultaneously challenging his teammates to improve defensively. The pitchers can be used as runners on singles to the outfield as well. Running from first to third on a base hit to right can be even more beneficial to the pitcher and to his team than scoring on a double, because taking the extra base can eliminate the double-play possibility and set up the opportunity for the pitcher to score on a fly ball hit to the outfield.

CHAPTER 9

CORRECTING
FLAWS

DRILL #87: CORRECTING THE STRIDE WITH A SHOESTRING

Objective: To help the pitcher develop a consistent and functional stride; to help the pitcher who has an exaggerated open stride or an exaggerated closed stride by helping him line up his stride foot with the target and his push-off foot.

Description: A simple shoestring is the teaching tool. If the pitcher has trouble with his direction and consistency while striding, the shoestring is a tool worth trying. A consistent stride is one that is controlled by the pitcher whose foot lands in the same place on each pitch. A functional stride is one that allows the pitcher freedom of movement and is one that is directly aligned toward the target (i.e., his stride foot is placed between his push-off foot and the target). The push-off foot can be used to determine if the pitcher's stride is out of alignment. Some pitchers are effective with a slightly closed stride position. Others are better with a slightly open stride. Still others prefer to stride absolutely in a straight line toward the target. All three positions are acceptable, provided the desired stride is effective for that particular pitcher. Regardless of the style he uses, the pitcher should consistently place his stride foot in the same spot.

Using his push-off foot as a guide, the pitcher can determine whether he is a toe-to-toe, a toe-to-heel, or a toe-to-arch strider. If, for example, he desires to be a toe-to-arch strider, he should lineup the shoestring with the arch of his push-off foot, lay the shoestring out, and point it toward the target. When he strides to throw, the inside part of the pitcher's stride foot should be on the shoestring. A toe-to-toe stride requires that the shoestring be laid out in a line from the top of his push-off foot to the target. At the same time, the ball of his stride foot should be on the shoestring. The shoestring alignment for a toe-to-heel stride, on the other hand, involves laying the shoestring out from the heel of the stride foot toward the target.

This drill should be used for pitchers who experience problems with their strides. While the drill is certainly not a cure-all for all stride-related problems, it can be effective if the pitcher is serious about developing a functional and consistent stride.

DRILL #88: PREVENTING OVERSTRIDING WITH A MAT

Objective: To help the overstriding pitcher develop a shorter stride.

Description: The pitcher determines an appropriate stride for himself and then marks the spot where his stride foot would normally land. Next, he places a rubber mat, a piece of conveyor belt, a piece of carpet, or some other safe, soft material on the ground at the edge of the mark toward home plate. The pitcher then begins the drill by throwing to the target and striding short of the mat. Each time he steps on the mat, he has failed to shorten his stride. Until he learns to stride without hitting the mat, he has failed to correct his problem.

The pitcher should remove the mat when he can successfully and consistently stride without touching it. He should notice where his stride foot lands after the mat is removed. If, without using the mat as a reminder, the pitcher is able to stride in the correct spot, he no longer needs the mat. Under stress in game situations, however, he may begin to overstride again. If his overstriding cannot be cured, then the mat drill should be reintroduced. The pitcher should keep using the mat until he is able to solve his problem of overstriding.

DRILL #89: PREVENTING EXCESSIVELY OPEN STRIDING WITH A MAT

Objective: To help the pitcher keep from throwing with an exaggerated open stride, a movement that tends to interfere with his sense of balance and rhythm.

Description: The pitcher determines a functional stride for himself and marks that spot. A mat, a piece of conveyor belt, a piece of carpet, or some other soft, flat material is placed at the edge of that mark. The pitcher should not allow his stride foot to land on the mat. If his stride foot touches the mat during the throw, he has failed to correct his problem. He should continue to throw with the intent of striding directly at the target.

As soon as the pitcher is able to consistently stride to the correct (i.e., appropriate) spot, remove the mat. If the pitcher subsequently backslides and experiences the same problem, this drill should be employed again. The point to keep in mind is the fact that it is not unusual for a pitcher to revisit an old habit. If and when he does, appropriate corrective action should again be undertaken.

DRILL #90: IMPROVING THE PITCHER'S HEEL-OVER MOVEMENT WITH A BUCKET

Objective: To help the pitcher improve the heel-over movement after pushing off the rubber.

Description: The drill involves placing a small plastic bucket just outside the pitcher's throwing arm and in the area where his push-off foot performs its circular motion after releasing from the rubber. The pitcher may throw from either the stretch or the windup position. As a rule, the stretch position is recommended until the pitcher is successful with the drill. In this drill, the pitcher starts on the pitching rubber. He throws to a catcher. As his push-off foot releases from the rubber, the push-off foot should lift and circle the bucket. The pitcher should then complete the circle by bringing the push-off foot in contact with the ground in front of the bucket and turning the heel over.

This drill is particularly beneficial for those pitchers who drag their push-off foot or who have a lazy lift-and-circle motion. As the drill is executed properly, the pitcher must lift and circle his push-off foot, or he will hit the bucket.

DRILL #91: PREVENTING CLOSED STRIDING WITH A MAT

Objective: To help keep the pitcher from throwing across his body; to help the pitcher get his stride foot down in a direct line toward the target so that his throwing motion is not restricted.

Description: The pitcher should determine a correct stride for himself and mark that spot. A mat, piece of conveyor belt, or other soft, flat material should be placed at the edge of that spot. The task for the pitcher is to stride without touching the mat. The mat serves as a physical reminder for the pitcher. Repetition and commitment will help the mat drill work successfully. This drill may need to be employed several times over a period of time if the pitcher's problem with closed striding is too severe.

DRILL #92: DISCOURAGING EXCESSIVE DRAGGING OF PUSH-OFF FOOT WITH A PAPER CUP

Objective: To help the pitcher notice when he drags his push-off foot too far toward home plate.

Description: A simple paper cup is the teaching tool. The drill is particularly designed for the pitcher who drags his push-off foot in an extreme manner. The drill involves placing a paper cup at a distance approximately eight to 12 inches from the rubber, toward home plate, and in alignment with the toe of the pitcher's push-off foot.

By taking care to push off and lift his push-off foot over the paper cup, the pitcher can eliminate the dragging action of his foot and provide a more powerful push-off. This drill is designed to help the pitcher produce better angles with the top part of his body.

DRILL #93: CORRECTING AN INVERTED PUSH-OFF MOVEMENT

Objective: To correct a flaw that some pitchers develop as their foot pushes from the rubber that involves the pitcher disengaging his foot from the pitching rubber incorrectly and dragging and inverting it, instead of releasing and lifting it. (Note: This unusual, flawed movement throws the pitcher's push-off foot in the opposite direction before he circles and finishes with his push-off foot. In turn, such a movement interferes with the pitcher's balance and disrupts his timing. It also throws the pitcher out of alignment).

Description: The drill involves placing a paper cup or plastic milk-shake container in front of the middle of the back heel of the pitcher's push-off foot. The cup should be set approximately three inches in front. The pitcher begins the drill with his push-off foot in the stretch position and in contact with the pitching rubber. The pitcher then begins to throw to the catcher. While throwing, his major focus should be to make the proper release, circle, and heel-over motion with his push-off foot. The paper cup is placed there as a reminder. Should the pitcher push-off incorrectly, he will hit the container. If he executes the move correctly, he will not hit the cup. If the cup is knocked over, the pitcher should reset the cup and should keep working on this drill until his motion is corrected.

DRILL #94: ACHIEVING MAXIMUM ARM AND UPPER-BODY EXTENSION

Objective: To enhance the ability of the pitcher to achieve maximum extension of his throwing arm and upper body toward the plate as he directs his delivery at the target.

Description: A towel or sock and a chair are needed. The towel is folded lengthwise. The width of the towel should be approximately two inches. The center of the towel should be looped under the index and middle fingers. The pitcher should use his thumb to hold the towel in place. A sanitary sock can be used instead of the towel. If it is, a loop should be made at the foot end of the sanitary sock and grip the sanitary sock at the loop.

A chair should be placed in front of the pitcher, with the seat facing the pitcher. The placement of the chair is important. Before setting the chair in front of the pitcher, a positioning mark should be determined by assessing the pitcher's height and then adding four feet to the total. That distance should provide a relative benchmark for the area between the pitcher's push-off foot and the front edge of the chair seat. In the drill, the pitcher's task is to stride, make a throwing motion, and hit the front edge of the chair with the towel or sanitary sock. The towel or sanitary sock adds about 20 inches to the pitcher's reach. With proper alignment and full extension with his arm, upper body, and the towel, the pitcher should be able to gain a distance that equals the length of his body plus four feet.

If the pitcher is to hit the chair with the towel, his angles become critical. The rest of his mechanics can also be important factors in reaching the chair. If the pitcher recoils or loses his balance, for example, he will not be able to perform this drill properly.

In his efforts to reach the chair, the pitcher should avoid overstriding. Although pitchers have a tendency to try to reach the chair by lengthening their stride, this action is counterproductive. The pitcher's primary objective should be to maximally extend his upper body and his throwing lever. Overstriding generally creates a shorter lever. If the stride is too long, the pitcher's top half cannot extend and finish the throwing action. While this drill is an excellent teaching tool, it requires close supervision. As such, the coach should make sure the pitcher stays focused on adhering to the proper mechanics.

DRILL #95: ENHANCING A PITCHER'S LEVEL OF BALANCE AND THRUST WITH A PITCHING SCREEN

Objective: To help the pitcher keep his sense of balance and enhance his level of thrust and alignment.

Description: This drill involves the use of a large protective screen (preferably 6' x 8' or 8' x 8'). The ideal protective screen is a net screen that is heavy enough to remain stable during throwing drills. The net protects the ball and acts as a sort of built-in retrieval system. The screen can be of great help to a pitcher who is working on his throwing fundamentals. A regular or specific part of the throwing motion, for instance, can be practiced and repeated as often as is necessary to gain results.

One of the most positive features of the screen is that it does not talk. It does not say, as the catcher often does, "Get the ball over." The screen affords the pitcher the opportunity to work on specifics in relation to his mechanics without concern for control—a factor that can be extremely important when correcting or refining a difficult or poorly understood movement.

The pitcher should be encouraged to work independently on the screen in order to improve his sense of self-reliance. The drill entails throwing to the screen, which is an independent and individual endeavor. It allows the pitcher the opportunity to repeat a movement or series of movements enough times to obtain a sufficient sense of the proper "feel" for a particular movement. Furthermore, because he is only 15 to 20 feet from the screen and is not required to throw at top speed, the pitcher is able to make many throws.

Another advantage of using the screen is that a pitching coach can station himself on the opposite side of the screen and can achieve a front view of the pitcher. All factors considered, at this short range, and in this favorable position, the coach is better able to evaluate and instruct.

DRILL #96: CORRECTING THROWING ARM AND FOLLOW-THROUGH DIRECTION WITH A PAPER CUP

Objective: To help the pitcher who has trouble properly finishing his throwing motion.

Description: A simple paper cup is the teaching tool. The drill involves using a paper cup to become a target for the pitcher's hand at follow-through. If at follow-through the pitcher's throwing hand is in the area of the cup, then he has extended properly. He has arched his chest and bent his back. His stride leg has completed its push-off. The right-to-left action of his throwing arm has been completed. If the pitcher's hand is not in the immediate area of the cup, then he has not properly finished his throwing motion. As such, he should repeat the drill and make appropriate adjustments in his motion.

This drill is an "upgrade" of a traditional drill. The traditional drill required the pitcher to reach down and pick up dirt after finishing the pitch. The paper cup gives a better visual picture of the proper arc of the throwing arm at the finish of the throw.

CHAPTER 10

STUFF

DRILL #97: GRIP AND FINGER PRESSURE

Objective: To provide the pitcher with the opportunity to examine, experiment, and discover how to create effective pitches by using different grips and varying levels of finger pressure.

Description: Each pitcher is unique. As such, the same grip used by two different pitchers will not create the same results. The factors that can contribute to such a disparity are numerous, including finger length, wrist movement, hand strength, and flexibility of the thumb—all of which are unique to a particular pitcher. Therefore, it is important for each pitcher to develop an understanding of what works best for him.

This drill is done in the bullpen. It really amounts to spending a few minutes focusing on how to make the ball move; it calls for experimentation. The coach and the catcher can play important roles. The pitcher throws a series of pitches, trying to get the ball to move in a specific manner. The coach and the catcher, meanwhile, make mental notations that can help the pitcher accomplish his task.

The pitcher should attempt to throw the fastball with a sinker spin. As he experiments with finger pressure, he will find the grip and release that create the best results. Next, he should apply pressure to the outside of the ball and try to get the ball to rotate from right to left (for a right-handed pitcher). Again, careful observations made by the catcher and the coach can be very helpful to the pitcher.

Through this experimentation drill, the pitcher should learn to have a better sense of touch and feel with the baseball. It does not mean, however, that he necessarily changes the way he throws any of his pitches. It may, however, help him to refine the way he throws a particular pitch.

DRILL #98: ENHANCING FRONT-ARM USE WITH SURGICAL CORD

Objective: To help those pitchers who have difficulty in properly using their front arms.

Description: The front arm is a very important factor in a pitcher's delivery. A pitcher's front arm should reach out to the target. It is also a measuring stick for distance and direction. The front arm must be brought back into the body. As such, it should supply the pitcher with some degree of balance. It should also help his throwing arm gain extension. Furthermore, the front arm should help the throwing arm complete the throwing action. In reality, pitchers with dead or ineffective front arms never maximize their potential. Because they often struggle with their balance, they often find it hard to develop a consistent release point. Moreover, their dead front arms encourage recoiling.

A surgical cord can be used to improve the pitcher's front-arm action. The drill involves affixing a two-foot-long cord to a fence or any stationary object. The cord should be at chin level to the pitcher when the pitcher is in his stationary stride position. The pitcher begins the drill in his stationary stride position while holding the cord in his extended front hand. The pitcher's front hand is approximately two feet from the affixed end of the cord, an action that takes the slack out of the cord. As his throwing arm goes forward to simulate the throw, the pitcher should pull the cord in and, at the same time, brush his front-arm elbow against his rib cage. In order to perform this drill properly, the pitcher should make sure that the back of his glove reaches toward the target. It is from this position that the pitcher begins the drill. Next, he turns his thumb over while holding the cord with his fingers. He then elevates the heel of his front hand and pulls the cord directly in and brushes his front-arm rib cage with his elbow and hand.

DRILL #99: ACHIEVING PROPER CURVEBALL ROTATION

Objective: To help the pitcher develop a tight-spin curveball.

Description: This drill is conducted either in the bullpen or on flat ground. If the drill is done in the bullpen, each pitcher should throw to a catcher. If the drill is performed on flat ground, the pitchers should throw to each other. All factors considered, however, working on flat ground is preferable during the early stages of learning to throw the curveball.

The flat-ground portion of the drill calls for each pitcher to throw from a stationary-stride position. The pitchers should start at a distance of 30 or 40 feet. The distance should be increased to 60 feet as the pitcher learns to impart spin on the ball. From the lesser distance, the pitcher should work on getting his throwing arm up and into an angle that will get his fingers on top of the ball. Imagining that he is loaded at a clock, the pitcher should try to get curveballs to spin with a 12-to-6 rotation. This drill is a good way to teach the pitcher to get the feel of making the ball spin forward, although a forward spin is not necessarily the desired rotation for each pitcher. In fact, each pitcher should experiment with the curveball rotation until he finds the spin that is most effective for him. As the pitcher learns to create spin, he should concentrate on his grip and his release point—always making mental notations. As he makes mental notes, develops the feel, and learns how to apply pressure to the ball, his curveball will begin to take shape.

Next, the drill should be moved to the bullpen. In the bullpen, the pitcher should practice throwing the curveball from both the windup and the stretch. Developing the spin on a curveball takes a good deal of work. Once the drill is moved to the bullpen, the catcher should help the pitcher by offering suggestions and encouragements.

DRILL #100: PITCHOUT

Objective: To provide an opportunity for the pitcher to practice, develop, and maintain the proper techniques for a pitchout.

Description: On the surface, the pitchout appears to be a simple task. As such, many individuals erroneously conclude that a pitchout should be a simple and routine throw. In reality, however, it is not. For a pitchout to be successful, several factors are important. For example, the pitcher must deliver the ball to the plate faster than his normal pitches, and it must be far enough outside the strike zone to prevent the hitter from making contact with it. Furthermore, it must be high enough to place the catcher in a good throwing position.

Because the pitchout is not an easy pitch to throw, it needs to be practiced. It is important to practice the pitchout drill from the mound. The catcher is a vital part of this drill. As such, he should be in his normal position.

The drill involves having the pitchers form a line behind the mound. Each pitcher should be properly warmed up and ready to throw at his regular speed. In this drill, each pitcher takes his turn by throwing four pitches. Each pitch will be timed. Obviously, the pitcher is in the stretch position. The clock starts on the pitcher's first movement from the stretch and stops when the ball contacts the catcher's mitt. The time should be 1.3 seconds or faster.

On a pitchout, the pitcher's delivery should not be dramatically different from his normal delivery. The delivery does have some differences—although they should be as subtle as possible. These differences occur from the point the pitcher separates his hands to his follow-through. Instead of separating the hands and bottoming out, for instance, the pitcher lifts his throwing hand into the throwing position as would an infielder. He also lifts his stride leg but places it down more quickly than in his regular delivery. If the beginning of his leg lift and the height of his leg are the same as in his normal leg lift, he can quicken his delivery by shortening the arc of his throwing arm and the quickness of his stride. By this time, the baserunner has already decided to run or to stay at the base.

For best results, the pitcher should throw one pitch using a regular delivery and one pitch using a pitchout delivery. He should use timing and technique to get the ball to home plate quickly, about one-tenth of a second faster than the normal delivery. Because one of the keys is persistence, the pitcher should repeat this process several times. His ultimate goal should be to combine the proper technique with a quicker delivery to home.

Although the catcher gives the target on normal pitches, his job on a pitchout is initially to move his feet together and then move outside when the pitcher begins his throw. This movement puts the catcher in a favorable position to throw. By closing his feet together, the catcher can cover more distance and still maintain his balance. By increasing his range, the catcher gives the pitcher a bigger area in which to throw.

DRILL #101: RUNDOWN FOR PITCHERS

Objective: To teach the pitcher the fundamentals of rundown plays between first and second base and home plate and third base.

Description: This drill is a team exercise in which all the players, except the outfielders, assume their respective positions. The outfielders act as baserunners. The pitchers divide into two groups. Two separate plays are practiced simultaneously. One of the pitchers throws to first base, catching the runner in a rundown. This pitcher covers first and becomes involved in the rundown if the first baseman needs help. Each pitcher in that particular line practices this drill.

Meanwhile, a pitcher in the other line throws to the catcher. The catcher arm-fakes to second base and then throws to third base, where he gets the runner at third in a rundown. The pitcher who threw home covers home and backs up the catcher in the rundown. After each pitcher has taken a turn in a specific line, the pitchers alternate lines.

The purpose of this book is to provide many different tools to help pitchers and coaches. Although drills are merely supplements to both the coaches and the pitcher, when they are performed with commitment and attention to detail, they can be great assets to both. Of course, improvement hinges on repetition and hard work. The success of any drill depends on the way it is executed. On the other hand, it would be relatively foolish to conclude that merely performing a drill is the complete solution to any problem. When the drill fits the problem, and the performers in the drill are committed to solving that problem to the degree humanly possible, then the drill can have a positive impact on the pitcher's ability to perform to the best of his natural capabilities.

ABOUT THE AUTHOR

Bob Bennett is one of the winningest Division I coaches of all time. With on overall collegiate mark of 1,083 wins, Bennett has established himself as one of collegiate baseball's all-time great coaches. He ranks 11th on the NCAA all-time victory list and 6th among active coaches in wins.

Since first taking over as Fresno State's head coach 29 years ago, the Bulldogs have enjoyed constant success on the field of play, winning or sharing 16 league or division titles, advancing to the NCAA playoffs 19 times, and making trips to the College World Series in 1988 and 1991. His teams are consistently ranked in the National Top 25 polls. The Bulldogs have averaged nearly 40 wins per season, and Bennett himself has earned league College Coach of the Year honors 13 times, in addition to being named 1988 NCAA Coach of the Year by *The Sporting News.*

Bennett, who was inducted into the American Baseball Coaches Hall of Fame in 1992, has also been heavily involved in baseball at the international level, serving as head coach of the U.S. National Team in 1983 and 1986 and serving on the National Team's coaching staff in 1977 and 1979.

Considered one of the nation's top pitching coaches, Bennett is known for his fundamentally sound ball clubs. Bennett has seen nearly 200 of his players signed to professional contracts. Seven of his players have been first round-regular phase draft selections. In 29 years of Division I success, Coach Bennett's efforts have produced 24 All Americans. Eleven of these All Americans were pitchers. Collectively, his pitching staff has achieved a combined earned run average of 3.5, averaging over 450 strikeouts per season and eight strikeouts per game. Eleven of Bennett's pitchers have pitched for the U.S. National Team. In 30 years of teaching the fundamentals of pitching at Fresno State, Bennett has developed nearly one major league pitcher every two years. Thirteen of his pitchers have pitched in the major leagues.

Bennett served as President of the American Baseball Coaches Association in 1987 and is still an active board member of that organization. He and his wife, Karen, have three children, Karen, Brad, and Todd, and eight grandchildren.